Spiritual Contemplation of Christ's Suffering – A Lenten Devotion

Written by: Rev. Marcus Baikie, Rev. Jacob Benson, Rev. Travis Berg, Rev. Paul Cain, Rev. Neil Carlson, Rev. Rene Castillero, Rev. Timothy Fitzner, Rev. Joshua Scheer

Editor: Rev. Joshua Scheer
Cover Art: Rev. Roberto Rojas Jr.

ISBN: 9798876641267

Scripture quotations are from the ESV® Bible ("The Holy Bible," English Standard Version®), copyright ® 2001 by Crossway, a publishing ministry of Good News Publishers. Used by permission. All rights reserved.

Scripture in the Appendix is taken from the New King James Version®. Copyright © 1982 by Thomas Nelson. Used by permission. All rights reserved.

Hymn texts are public domain, unless otherwise noted.

Digital images were provided courtesy of Pitts Theology Library, Candler School of Theology, Emory University.

Pastors are encouraged to share, download, print, and use these publications within their congregations. Go to our website for PDFs of these devotions and other resources.

Printed copies of this resource are available for purchase on Amazon courtesy of Steadfast Press.

Copyright © 2024 by Steadfast Lutherans, Inc.
www.steadfastlutherans.org

STEADFAST PRESS
Believe. Teach. Confess.

*To the glory of our Triune God
and for the Evangelical Lutheran Church
wherever she is found.*

Introduction

> Jesus, I will ponder now
> On Your holy passion;
> With Your Spirit me endow
> For such meditation.
> Grant that I in love and faith
> May the image cherish
> Of Your suff'ring, pain, and death
> That I may not perish. (LSB 440:1)

Many people have throughout history done a lot of work on the suffering and death of Jesus Christ. Some of these works can be helpful. Some have been just wrong. This devotion is designed to be a help to you this Lent.

The matter of hearing and studying our Lord's passion is not just one of memorizing facts and events. It isn't about just knowing the horrors of the act of crucifixion or Judeo-Roman political relations. Those things can all add to our knowledge of the texts and help us understand what they mean, but the fruitful use of these text is to ponder them as the hymn stanza cited above states. That we, with love and faith would cherish the suffering, pain, and death of Jesus that we would not perish eternally. That is, by faith trusting that Christ Jesus did all of that for you and for your salvation.

The appendix of this devotion includes a harmony of the passion of our Lord, an arrangement of texts from the four Gospels in a good order to read them all together. They are a record of the history of our Lord's suffering and death. This is what the fullness of time is about – the record of God's faithfulness to His promises. His promises meant for you and made to you. Take some time to look through the texts, read them. Be familiar with the history of our Lord's suffering and death. Once you have these objective things down, you can make a start at making them "for you". That is a fruitful exercise and use of these days and texts in your households.

Our whole Lenten devotion will focus on the suffering of Jesus for your sake. The various aspects of this spiritual contemplation set up for each week are meant to strengthen your faith in Jesus by showing you just what God accomplished for you in the suffering and death of Christ for you.

Each week is arranged around a central theme for the week and is announced on the Sunday that begins the week. The week then uses Old Testament, Psalm, Epistle, and Gospel lessons to teach that certain aspect. An added contemplation is to be found in each Saturday devotion as we learn the seven classic virtues from Christ's suffering as well. In this way we find our whole life as Christians can be benefited by such contemplation of Christ and what He has done for us.

May this devotion benefit you and your households. May it strengthen your faith in Jesus and your love for your neighbor, for whom our Lord also suffered. May it give you instruction in godliness that as the Spirit makes you able, you would walk in the virtues perfectly possessed and practiced by our Lord for our sake.

Rev. Joshua V. Scheer
Steadfast Lutherans

Ash Wednesday
Matthew 6:1-6, 16-21

" "And when you fast, do not look gloomy like the hypocrites, for they disfigure their faces that their fasting may be seen by others. Truly, I say to you, they have received their reward. But when you fast, anoint your head and wash your face, that your fasting may not be seen by others but by your Father who is in secret. And your Father who sees in secret will reward you." (Matthew 6:16–18, ESV)

Today is the beginning of the season of Lent. The season has historically been one of penitence and discipline for Christians. This brings to mind the ancient disciplines of prayer, fasting, and almsgiving – three Christian disciplines taught by our Lord in Matthew 6 and elsewhere. Each of these has been pictured in history as fighting against a particular enemy of our souls – prayer, the devil – fasting, our flesh – and almsgiving, the world.

All three of these disciplines were not only taught but also practiced by our Lord Himself. These were a part of His active obedience to the Law and earning a true, perfect righteousness for us. This is the righteousness that we possess by faith in Him. It is the righteousness that avails before God in heaven.

In teaching and doing these things our Lord taught us about discipline for ourselves. This discipline never earns salvation or God's favor. Instead it helps us to curb our sinful nature and to place our trust in Christ. It helps us in our Christian lives.

Christ did these things in the flesh. By that we have a righteousness that God sees and is pleased with. We are righteous because Christ makes us this way. Because of that, we learn to discipline our flesh as well.

This Lent, set more tine aside for prayer. Set some food aside to teach your body it doesn't control you. Set money aside to help someone less fortunate, even if the world would scratch its head at such unseen generosity.

Lord Jesus, You alone are our Savior. By Your obedience, suffering, and death we have eternal life. Because You have done this for us, help us to see the value in practicing discipline ourselves during this season of Lent. In Your Name we pray. Amen.

Thursday after Ash Wednesday
Galatians 4:4-7

"But when the fullness of time had come, God sent forth his Son, born of woman, born under the law, to redeem those who were under the law, so that we might receive adoption as sons." (Galatians 4:4–5, ESV)

Through this entire Lenten series you will be asked to listen, read, focus upon, and pray with certain aspects of our Lord's suffering in mind. The most fruitful reading of any of this is to make sure you read all these things as being done by God for you and for your salvation. Yes, this divine work and divine revelation of it is for you.

As mentioned in the introduction, the appendix of this devotion includes a harmony of the passion of our Lord, an arrangement of texts from the four Gospels in a good order to read them all together. They are a record of the history of our Lord's suffering and death. This is what the fullness of time is about – the record of God's faithfulness to His promises. His promises meant for you and made to you. Take some time to look through the texts, read them. Be familiar with the history of our Lord's suffering and death. Once you have these objective things in mind, you can make a start at making them "for you". That is a fruitful exercise and use of these days and texts in your households.

In the text today, to "redeem" is purchasing language. As we are taught in the Small Catechism, our Lord Jesus Christ redeems us not with gold or silver, but with His holy precious blood by His innocent suffering and death. This was set up before time by our loving God. The entire Trinity had this plan in place for our salvation, for your salvation. All of history has followed the course set for it by God. A course bent on your salvation. The Lord has by His suffering and death redeemed you. As you ponder betrayals, accusations, torture, and death through the suffering of Jesus, may you realize that this is what He has done for your redemption.

Lord Jesus Christ, we give You thanks for the gift of Your Word. Help us to hear it, learn it, and gain trust in You from it, that in the end we obtain Your goal in giving it to us – the salvation of our souls. Amen.

Friday after Ash Wednesday
1 Corinthians 1:18-2:5

"For I decided to know nothing among you except Jesus Christ and him crucified." (1 Corinthians 2:2, ESV)

The Apostle Paul has a zeroed in focus on Christ crucified. The suffering and death of our Lord Jesus Christ was central to all of his preaching and teaching. In the text today we learn that this is because it is how God has chosen to act and reveal Himself to us. If this is how God wants to reveal Himself, then we would do well to dig deeper than just outward facts or even inward emotions. The goal here is faithful, spiritual contemplation of our Lord's suffering.

When you hear people today ignore Christ, seek to equivocate Him with other spiritualities, or even mock Him, realize this is exactly what the Apostle encountered in His travels for the sake of the Gospel. The word of the cross - the Word of Christ's suffering and death for the sake of sinners is foolishness to most sinners, who being already death in their sins, have no concern for true spiritual life. It is also a stumblingblock to others because the Word of Cross is so offensive on so many levels. It's too simple for some. It doesn't give us anything to do for others. It's offensive that God would die for His enemies. It doesn't make sense according to any worldly way of thinking. Paul's proclamation here is personal. He knows what it was to be called a fool, a heretic, a false teacher for insisting upon Jesus Christ, the LORD, being crucified for the sake of sinners who could not help themselves.

Perhaps the crucifixion has been offensive to you in many ways. Perhaps you are so familiar with the story that you are toying with contempt for it. Perhaps you get to distracted in the many rabbit trails leading away from the work of Christ at Calvary. Perhaps you don't want to see the horrible death of Jesus as being necessary because of what you did today, or yesterday, or will do tomorrow. This Lent is time to repent of any and all of that and turn once again and take on the mindset of Paul – be determined to know Christ crucified and be blessed in trusting in Him and His work for your salvation. If others are upset by that, consider it a blessing – just as Jesus promised it is.

Lord Jesus, Your work of our salvation is the greatest work ever done. Help us to keep You and Your work at the center of our thoughts, words, and deeds during this Lenten season and for all of our days. Amen.

Saturday after Ash Wednesday
1 Corinthians 16:13-14

"Be watchful, stand firm in the faith, act like men, be strong. Let all that you do be done in love." (1 Corinthians 16:13–14, ESV)

The Virtue of Courage

Saint Ambrose (4th centuary bishop of Milan) teaches us that, apart from the three Theological Virtues of Faith, Hope, and Love (1 Corinthians 13:13), we also glean from the ancient pagans the idea of four cardinal virtues: temperance, justice, prudence, and courage. More profoundly than simply saying Christians must follow these virtues, Ambrose tells us that the virtues find their perfection in the "hypostatic union." That is to say, it is in the person of Christ – a full divinity which has found a personal union with full humanity – that we learn to live virtuous lives. Thus, on these Saturdays in Lent, as we prepare our bodies and minds for the Lord's Supper and the Lord's Word, we will ask ourselves how Christ embodies these seven virtues, and how He teaches us to imitate Him.

The fourth Cardinal Virtue, courage, is derived from a Greek word that simply means "manly." This is the same word Saint Paul uses to exhort the Corinthians to good living, not merely "being courageous," but specifically "acting like men." This is not a call to brutishness but is hedged in and interpreted by the following sentence: let all that you do be done in love. Christ was no brute when He made his way to the cross, but was a courageous lamb, led to the slaughter without opening His mouth. He did not die to spite His enemies, but He embodied perfect fortitude dying for the whole world, but especially for His bride the Church – thus showing all men how to live and die for their wives: being prepared to make the ultimate sacrifice, shedding all cowardliness, and acting like men to protect those nearest them, knowing that Christ has already died to protect their souls from hell.

O Jesus Christ, true man, born of the Virgin in this age: remind us that as You participate in our humanity, we also are called to participate in Your manliness. Give us hearts of fortitude, minds of courage, and words of love, that all we say and do in this life would shed light on the courageous sacrifice You made for the whole world on the altar of the cross. For You live and reign with the Father and the Holy Ghost, ever one God, world without end.

Temptation of Jesus (Matthew 4)

First Sunday in Lent
Matthew 4:1-11

"Then Jesus was led up by the Spirit into the wilderness to be tempted by the devil. And after fasting forty days and forty nights, he was hungry." (Matthew 4:1–2, ESV)

"The obedience of Christ for our righteousness"

Today we ponder Christ's obedience. Lententide is devoted to the end of Jesus' earthly life, but we must begin at Christmas time to understand Christ's obedience properly. "(Jesus) emptied himself, by taking the form of a servant, being born in the likeness of men" (Philippians 2:7 ESV). In order to save all men Jesus had to become like all men. He had to perform a task mankind was unable to complete. Jesus had to fulfill the Law. God demanded perfection from His people. Any failure resulted in death (cf. Romans 6:23 ESV). To overcome death one must keep the Law, the whole Law, perfectly and undefiled. Jesus was born for this purpose. The sinless One, born of a virgin, kept the Law to fulfill the Law. Joseph and Mary took Jesus, as a babe, to Jerusalem to do for Him as the Law required (cf. Luke 2:22-32). He lived a sinless life, obedient to the Father's will in every aspect.

Our Lord was baptized into repentance for the forgiveness of sins (cf. Matthew 3:13-17). The sinless One was in no need of repentance. Yet He was baptized by John to fulfill all righteousness. It is said, "Jesus was baptized into our dirty bathwater." Which means, He had no need of baptism, but in submitting to baptism He took our sin upon himself. In doing so He left the water clean. Thus, purifying baptism and making it a life-giving flood.

After His baptism the Spirit led Jesus into the wilderness. Again, our Lord was obedient to the will of God. There He was tempted for forty days and forty nights. Never did He fall. Unlike the first Adam, our Lord remained faithful to the will of God. Jesus has done for us what we could never do for ourselves. He has fulfilled the Law in our stead.

Heavenly Father, as we sit in sackcloth and ashes mourning our sinfulness grant us faith to acknowledge our failure and to trust in Jesus' obedience to You, that we may dwell in His righteousness all the days of our lives; through the same Jesus Christ, our Lord. Amen.

Monday, Lent 1
Isaiah 50:5-10

"Behold, the Lord GOD helps me; who will declare me guilty? Behold, all of them will wear out like a garment; the moth will eat them up. Who among you fears the LORD and obeys the voice of his servant? Let him who walks in darkness and has no light trust in the name of the LORD and rely on his God." (Isaiah 50:9–10, ESV)

Lutherans often speak of forensic justification. It is best explained as a courtroom. God sits on the judgment seat. You are on trial for ALL of your sins. Yet, we do not sit in fear. A little glance over at your advocate Jesus lets you know you have nothing to fear. At which time Jesus stands up to plead your case. He admits your sinfulness. But then he tells the judge (Himself), yes Jesus will judge the world (John 5:29). (When your lawyer is also the judge, you know there is nothing to fear.) Jesus explains, He has taken your sin upon Himself. He has walked in your shoes for you. He has borne your burdens. Yes, without doubt you failed to keep the Law. But He came and kept the Law for you. He was faithful where you were not. He continues to explain that He also took your punishment for you. He was obedient to the point of death, even death on a cross (Philippians 2:8). Jesus has paid your debt. He has atoned for your sins. Thus, the Judge bangs the gavel and declares you righteous. He declares He sees no sin in you because Jesus took it from you. He sees no punishment to be rendered because Jesus has taken it already.

As the devil, the world, and even your own sinful flesh pick at your brain, telling you how wicked you are, do not let it drive you to despair. Confess your sins. Cry out that yes, you are wicked and guilty, but it is of no concern. Jesus has given you His righteousness. Jesus has declared you just. Jesus has done for you what you could never do for yourself. Those voices may harass you all your days on earth, but they will stop one day. And all you will hear is the voice of Jesus who has declared you righteous.

Heavenly Father, through the obedience of Your Son on the cross You have declared us just. Send your Spirit upon us that we may ever cling to this gospel in times of despair; though the same Jesus Christ, our Lord. Amen.

Tuesday, Lent 1
Romans 5:1-21

"For as by the one man's disobedience the many were made sinners, so by the one man's obedience the many will be made righteous." (Romans 5:19, ESV)

"All mankind fell in Adam's fall, One common sin infects us all. From one to all the curse descends, And over all God's wrath impends." (LSB 562:1). We live in a victimhood culture. We are accustomed to crying, "It's not my fault. Sure, I did it. But it because of …" We blame someone else for our disobedience. Some may think this is a new trend, but it's not. It's the same thing Adam and Eve did in the garden. "The woman, whom you have given to me" (Gen. 3:12) Adam blamed God for giving him the seductive temptress. The woman said, "The serpent deceived me" (Gen. 3:13). She blamed the devil. Try and blame another we might, but it does not work. Adam was guilty. Eve was guilty. We are guilty. We are responsible for our own actions. Falling to peer pressure does not remove the transgression. What does remove the transgression is the life and death of Jesus. His obedience to the Law fulfilled the Law. He never blamed anyone else. In fact, He did the opposite. He took on everyone else's blame. He bore our sin and shame. He lived as God desires all men to live. He lived a sinless life. Yet, He still died. The righteous and holy God-man still died. Death had no claim over Him however. It was only able to take Him because He bore our sin. He took our death. What a holy and righteous man is our Lord! He did as the Father desired and thus His righteousness is bestowed upon us. By Jesus' blood we have been made righteous. The one man Jesus Christ has broken the curse of death. He has given us life.

Holy Lord, we confess that we are sinful and unclean. We do not come to You on account of our own righteousness, but we call out to You because of Jesus' righteousness. Let His grace and mercy cover all of our sins, for which we are truly guilty. By the power of Your Spirit, grant us to walk in His paths all the days of our lives; though that same Jesus Christ, our Lord. Amen.

Wednesday, Lent 1
John 6:35-40

"For I have come down from heaven, not to do my own will but the will of him who sent me." (John 6:38, ESV)

I remember sitting in middle school learning about self-esteem. I also remember sitting at a district convention hearing Dr. Cameron MacKenzie teaching about the sinful problems the teaching on self-esteem has brought to the Church. Self-esteem builds a person up and causes them to boast in themselves. It clashes profusely with the Biblical teaching on our sinful condition. We are sinful and unclean; lost and condemned creatures. There is no good in us. We do not fear God, love Him, seek Him, or desire to do His will. We should not think God dwells with man because of any merit or worthiness in man. God dwelt with man because of who God is. He is love (1 John 4:16). We should despair of ourselves and thank God for deigning to dwell with such unworthy creatures.

"What motivated Christ to die and make full payment for your sins? His great love for His Father and for me and other sinners, as it is written in John 14; Romans 5; Galatians 2; and Ephesians 5." (Small Catechism, Christian Questions with Their Answers, 17). It is Jesus' love of God the Father that causes Him to become man and walk among such unworthy beings. His willingness to do whatever the Father desires causes Him to do the most wonderful acts. His willing obedience causes the holy to touch the unholy. To make Himself unclean. To suffer all, even hell. All this Jesus did out of love for His Father. All this He did out of love for us also. Though we are completely undeserving of His love He loves us anyway. What joy and comfort there is in knowing God's salvation comes from Him, apart from us. Our salvation isn't dependent upon anything we have done. It is fully and completely dependent upon who God is. In humbling Himself to fulfill the Father's will Jesus has lifted us up. If we have any reason to boast it is in Christ Jesus.

Lord God Almighty, teach us to despair of ourselves and find comfort only in the undeserved grace of Your Son. Grant us to walk in the humility of Jesus being guided not by our own wills, but Yours; through the same Jesus Christ, our Lord. Amen.

Thursday, Lent 1
Psalm 16

"The LORD is my chosen portion and my cup; you hold my lot." (Psalm 16:5, ESV)

The cup of death is full of the curse. It brims over and destroyed any whom it touches. Our Lord Jesus willingly drank of it. He prayed for the Father to take it away, but nevertheless, He put doing the Father's will first (cf. Luke 22:42). The Father's will was for Jesus to drink the cup. For it to be poured over His head and drip down His body until it puddled upon the earth. Jesus silently and willingly went to the slaughter (cf. Isaiah 53:7). He not only put the cup to His lips, but He drank it all. Jesus drank our cup of death. He suffered our curse. It poured down his body in the form of blood. From the crown of thorns piercing His brow, down His face. From His pierced hands, down His arms. From His pierced side, down His body. From His feet, down the cross. When His blood pooled upon the ground at Golgotha it did not pool into the curse of death. It formed the pool of life. Jesus drank the cup of death and out of it poured the cup of life. As His blood flowed from His body it filled another cup; the cup of life. This cup our Lord gives us to drink. "The cup of blessing that we bless, is it not a participation in the blood of Christ? The bread that we break, is it not a participation in the body of Christ?" (1 Corinthians 10:16 ESV). Jesus took the cup of death for us, that He might give us the cup of life. He has fulfilled the Father's will. He took our death and in its place He has given us life; eternal life. Death has been destroyed. Life has been won. He is our hope and our salvation. He gives us eternal life. But not a life forever here on this sinful earth. He gives us the cup of life here but also there, it is enjoyed in the kingdom of heaven. Through Jesus we inherit the Kingdom to come. We inherit paradise. Thus, eternal life will be lived in the new heaven and the new earth (cf. Rev. 21:1). The cup of life is full of salvation. That is the cup Jesus has given us to drink and it too is filled to the brim. It overflows with righteousness.

Heavenly Father, You sent Your Son to drink of death for us. He has fulfilled your will. He has given us life. Let us walk in that new life here on earth, keeping Your statues and commands that we may walk in that same life for all eternity in Your heavenly kingdom; through Jesus Christ, our Lord. Amen.

Friday, Lent 1
Hebrews 5:1-10

"In the days of his flesh, Jesus offered up prayers and supplications, with loud cries and tears, to him who was able to save him from death, and he was heard because of his reverence. Although he was a son, he learned obedience through what he suffered. And being made perfect, he became the source of eternal salvation to all who obey him, being designated by God a high priest after the order of Melchizedek." (Hebrews 5:7–10, ESV)

Our Lord Jesus fulfilled the Law in our stead. He was obedient to the Father's commands in every way. Jesus was also obedient to the Father's will in terms of our salvation. Jesus allowed Himself to suffer and die for us. He made it clear that at any time He wanted He could have called down legions of angels to defend Him (cf. Matthew 26:53-54). But He did not. Jesus wanted to do the Father's will. Jesus wanted to save us. Therefore, He sat silently by as He was arrested. He remained silent through a mock trial. He did not resist when the cross was thrown across His shoulders. He carried it with His beaten body as far as He was physically able. He then allowed Himself to be hoisted up upon the cross. There He hung, quietly and patiently, obedient to the point of death for our salvation.

In Jesus' life He was actively obedient to the Father in order to earn our salvation, through the Law. In His life He was also passively obedient to the Father in order to earn our salvation, becoming the gospel. Jesus fulfilled the law. That is the gospel. There is nothing for us to do. He has done it all. Jesus now gives away His work of salvation. Freely, by grace through faith, we receive the salvation Jesus earned for us. It is by this faith we are declared righteous. It is by Jesus' blood we are made righteous and by faith it is counted to us as righteousness. We have nothing to offer, because Jesus offered it all. He is our salvation.

Holy Lord, Holy and Most Gracious God, we give You thanks for declaring us righteous through the blood of Your Son. Send Your Spirit upon us that we may ever dwell in this faith to life everlasting. Grant Your Spirit also to sanctify us, that having been redeemed by Jesus was may be imitators of Him in thought, word, and deed; through that same Son, Jesus Christ, our Lord. Amen.

Saturday, Lent 1
1 Thessalonians 5:12-24

""Do not quench the Spirit. Do not despise prophecies, but test everything; hold fast what is good. Abstain from every form of evil. Now may the God of peace himself sanctify you completely, and may your whole spirit and soul and body be kept blameless at the coming of our Lord Jesus Christ." (1 Thessalonians 5:19–23, ESV)

The Virtue of Prudence

The second cardinal virtue that Christians are called to chase after is Prudence. Though we may hear words like "prude" or "prudish," this is not a selfish, and stuffy way of living. True prudence is about wise discernment of the things of the world. This is why Saint Paul tells the Christians at Thessalonica to "test everything." To be discerning and prudent is to be wise enough to test all things, to learn what is good and what is evil. In this life of discernment, Christians learn to not despise true prophecies, and in doing so they learn to hate false words spoken in the name of God.

Indeed, one of the prophecies of Christ specifically spoke of His prudence. Soon after Ahaz learned that a virgin would bear a son, he was also told that this virgin's son would know how to "refuse the evil and choose the good," (Isaiah 7:14-15). As a twelve year old boy, Jesus knew that He must be about His father's business. As a grown man, Jesus wept in the garden, asking for the cup of God's wrath to be taken away from Him. But knowing what was good, what was true, and what would result in beauty for all mankind, Jesus chose the good. He chose to suffer for the sins of the world, He chose to be beaten and mocked and derided, all so that His blood could be shed to atone for the sin of Adam, Eve, and everyone who can trace their lineage back to them.

Last Sunday, Christ taught us how to refuse the devil: by relying on the clear words of Holy Scripture. It is in this same written word that we learn to refuse the evil and choose the good in our daily lives. So return to the scriptures, cherish prophecies, test everything, and abstain from what is evil.

You have come to us Emmanuel, teach us to choose the good and to ever sing Your praise as You teach us how to live:
> **O come, Thou Wisdom, from on high,**
> **and order all things far and nigh;**
> **to us the *path of knowledge* show,**
> **and teach us in her ways to go. Amen.**

The Canaanite Woman (Matthew 15)

Second Sunday in Lent
Matthew 15:21-28

"She said, "Yes, Lord, yet even the dogs eat the crumbs that fall from their masters' table." Then Jesus answered her, "O woman, great is your faith! Be it done for you as you desire." And her daughter was healed instantly." (Matthew 15:27–28, ESV)

Christ's Suffering as a Payment and Sacrifice for Our Sin

When Jesus sent the Twelve out on their missionary journey in Matthew 10, He instructed them, "Go nowhere among the Gentiles and enter no town of the Samaritans, but go rather to the lost sheep of the house of Israel." Such language is echoed in our text: He answered, "I was sent only to the lost sheep of the house of Israel."

At Israel's rejection of Jesus, we see that these injunctions are only temporary. The final word on the matter in Matthew's Gospel account is," Go therefore and make disciples of all nations…" Our Lord's confirmation that He is to be Lord over all nations is fulfilling the Old Testament prophecies that disciples will be drawn to Him from the ends of the earth, a preview of the multitudes of every tribe and race and language seen in the book of Revelation.

Jesus answered her, "O woman, great is your faith! Be it done for you as you desire." And her daughter was healed instantly.

Johann Gerhard says that we should "view the suffering of Christ as a clear reflector of His heartfelt, burning love towards us" (*Explanation of the History of the Suffering and Death of Jesus*, p. 12). It is not being a descendant of Abraham that saves. It is not citizenship in a particular nation. Believe on the Lord Jesus with all your heart, soul, and mind. Trust Him. Pray in faith. Humble yourself completely before the Holy God. And be comforted that God's salvation is for all people, especially you.

O God, You see that of ourselves we have no strength. By Your mighty power defend us from all adversities that may happen to the body and from all evil thoughts that may assault and hurt the soul; through Jesus Christ, Your Son, our Lord, who lives and reigns with You and the Holy Spirit, one God, now and forever. Amen.

Monday, Lent 2
Isaiah 52:13-53:12

"Yet it was the will of the LORD to crush him; he has put him to grief; when his soul makes an offering for guilt, he shall see his offspring; he shall prolong his days; the will of the LORD shall prosper in his hand. Out of the anguish of his soul he shall see and be satisfied; by his knowledge shall the righteous one, my servant, make many to be accounted righteous, and he shall bear their iniquities. Therefore I will divide him a portion with the many, and he shall divide the spoil with the strong, because he poured out his soul to death and was numbered with the transgressors; yet he bore the sin of many, and makes intercession for the transgressors." (Isaiah 53:10–12, ESV)

Christ was pierced for our transgressions. His suffering was payment and sacrifice for all sin. Our sin. Gerhard writes that "we should view everything that happened to Christ in His suffering as if God Himself has done it" (p. 11).

The Lord sent the Son to save His people. That took suffering a cross to accomplish. The offering is made and accepted. Those who believe are His offspring. They prosper by being His witnesses to the ends of the earth, beginning in Jerusalem.

The light of life is yet to come. Easter Dawn shows the Son rising in the light of life. The servant is righteous, blameless. Death could not hold Him. Death cannot harm those He holds. Many are made right with God, because He bore their iniquities.

And He sits at the right hand of the Father. And He will come again with glory to judge both the living and the dead, whose kingdom will have no end. He is the intercessor between God and man.

God be merciful to us and bless us, and cause His face to shine upon us, and have mercy upon us. We adore You, O Lord, and we praise and glorify Your holy resurrection. For behold, by the wood of Your cross joy has come into all the world. Amen.

Tuesday, Lent 2
Galatians 3:10-14

"For all who rely on works of the law are under a curse; for it is written, "Cursed be everyone who does not abide by all things written in the Book of the Law, and do them." Now it is evident that no one is justified before God by the law, for "The righteous shall live by faith." But the law is not of faith, rather "The one who does them shall live by them." Christ redeemed us from the curse of the law by becoming a curse for us—for it is written, "Cursed is everyone who is hanged on a tree"— so that in Christ Jesus the blessing of Abraham might come to the Gentiles, so that we might receive the promised Spirit through faith." (Galatians 3:10–14, ESV)

The Law of God is misunderstood by many as a means of salvation. No. All who rely on works of the law for the purpose of salvation are under a curse. We cannot keep the law. We are disobedient sinners.

Gerhard reminds us of "how through the disobedience of one many became sinners; also how through the obedience of One many become righteous" (pp. 8-9). Galatians 3 teaches this clearly: "Cursed be everyone who does not abide by all things written in the Book of the Law to do them." This is the truth found in Deuteronomy 27:26, Jeremiah 11:3, and Ezekiel 18:4.

It is also true that "through the obedience of the One many become righteous." Christ Jesus is that One. Christ's suffering is payment and sacrifice for our sin. Galatians 3 also teaches that clearly: Christ redeemed us from the curse of the law by becoming a curse for us."

Therefore, the righteous shall live by faith. In Christ Jesus the blessing of Abraham has come to us Gentiles. We Christians have received the promised Holy Spirit through faith in Christ. The curse is over. The blessing of Christ endures forever.

Lord Jesus Christ, our Good Shepherd and Master, You languished on the cross in sorrow, mortal anguish for our sins. You inherited the wrath and woe we merited. We thank You for dying for us wandering sheep, servants who owe a debt of sin. Amen.

Wednesday, Lent 2
John 3:13-21

"Whoever believes in him is not condemned, but whoever does not believe is condemned already, because he has not believed in the name of the only Son of God. And this is the judgment: the light has come into the world, and people loved the darkness rather than the light because their works were evil. For everyone who does wicked things hates the light and does not come to the light, lest his works should be exposed. But whoever does what is true comes to the light, so that it may be clearly seen that his works have been carried out in God.""" (John 3:18–21, ESV)

These selected verses follow "For God So Loved the World." Gerhard writes that "we should remember what happened to Christ, the Head of the Church, [for] that is also what the members of this Body also have to be prepared for" (p. 13).

Christ's suffering is truly payment and sacrifice for the sin of the world. Yet, even though light has come into the world, some people still love the darkness rather than the light. Why? Their works are evil. They are embarrassed on some level. They are prideful and cannot bear rebuke. And they still do not want their evil works identified as evil. Such is the fallen world around us. Culture and civil law may at times call good "evil," and evil "good." That which is legal or popular can still be evil and utterly sinful in the eyes of God.

It is therefore judgement, the judgement of God, Himself that the light, Christ, has come into the world. Everyone who does wicked things hates the light, lest his evil become evident as evil and everyone would know it without a doubt.

In Christ, we come to the light in faith, believing in Him, trusting in Him. Jesus Christ is the light of the world, the light no darkness can overcome.

O God, You so loved us that you gave Your only begotten Son, Jesus Christ, to suffer, die, and rise for us, so that believing in Him as our Savior, we shall not perish but have everlasting life. Amen.

Thursday, Lent 2
Psalm 103

"He does not deal with us according to our sins, nor repay us according to our iniquities. For as high as the heavens are above the earth, so great is his steadfast love toward those who fear him; as far as the east is from the west, so far does he remove our transgressions from us. As a father shows compassion to his children, so the LORD *shows compassion to those who fear him. For he knows our frame; he remembers that we are dust. As for man, his days are like grass; he flourishes like a flower of the field; for the wind passes over it, and it is gone, and its place knows it no more." (Psalm 103:10–16, ESV)*

Johann Gerhard says that "we should see the passion history as a reflection of Christ's glorious virtues; that we see these virtues as a prescribed model and formula; that we also direct and pattern our life and sojourn after it" (p. 14).

Our faithful, steadfast, and loving Lord has preserved a faithful remnant through all of human history. "But the steadfast love of the Lord is from everlasting to everlasting on those who fear him, and his righteousness to children's children, to those who keep his covenant and remember to do his commandments" (verses 17-18).

The Lord knows well our frailty: "For he knows our frame; he remembers that we are dust. As for man, his days are like grass; he flourishes like a flower of the field; for the wind passes over it, and it is gone, and its place knows it no more" (verses 14-16).

In contrast, the Word of the Lord endures forever. God's promises to us in Christ endure forever. Christ's suffering as payment and sacrifice for sin needed to happen only once to endure forever. And that sacrifice has happened once for your sake and its benefit to you is forever.

Lord of the angels, send Your mighty ones to do Your word, that we may also obey the voice of Your word. Lord of angel hosts, equip Your ministers, to do Your will. Lord of all things, bless Your works in all places of Your dominion. Bless us body and soul for the sake of Christ. Amen. (Based on Psalm 103:20-22)

Friday, Lent 2
1 Peter 3:18-22

"For Christ also suffered once for sins, the righteous for the unrighteous, that he might bring us to God, being put to death in the flesh but made alive in the spirit, in which he went and proclaimed to the spirits in prison, because they formerly did not obey, when God's patience waited in the days of Noah, while the ark was being prepared, in which a few, that is, eight persons, were brought safely through water. Baptism, which corresponds to this, now saves you, not as a removal of dirt from the body but as an appeal to God for a good conscience, through the resurrection of Jesus Christ, who has gone into heaven and is at the right hand of God, with angels, authorities, and powers having been subjected to him." (1 Peter 3:18–22, ESV)

Christ is the Suffering Servant, the Sin-bearer, our Substitute, and He is the Reconciler between us and God. Jesus' Suffering on cross for our sake is recorded in Matthew 27:45-46. Jesus also descended into Hell, not to suffer, but to announce His victory over sin, death, and the devil. This took place between His burial and Resurrection.

There is no second chance for salvation after death. That is precluded by Hebrews 9:27-28: "And just as it is appointed for man to die once, and after that comes judgment, so Christ, having been offered once to bear the sins of many, will appear a second time, not to deal with sin but to save those who are eagerly waiting for him."

Baptism corresponds to God's rescue of Noah's family. We receive the benefits of this new life when the old Adam inside each of us is drowned in the waters of baptism and a new man arises, having put on Christ through faith. Gerhard writes that we should view Christ's suffering "as a payment and sacrifice for our manifold sin" (p. 10). Baptism now saves you because Jesus delivers salvation through baptism.

Lord God, through the washing of water with the Word we are one with Christ Jesus in His death and resurrection. Renew all who have been in Your Holy Spirit that we may live before You in righteousness and purity forever. Amen.

Saturday, Lent 2
1 John 5:1-5

"By this we know that we love the children of God, when we love God and obey his commandments. For this is the love of God, that we keep his commandments. And his commandments are not burdensome." (1 John 5:2–3, ESV)

The Virtue of Love

'The greatest of the theological virtues is Love, so says the Holy Spirit (1 Corinthians 13:13). More than any other word in the Bible, it is probably Love that has been twisted and redefined to make it into something else. Irenaeus (2nd century bishop) wrote long ago that heretics treated scripture in this way: they saw a mosaic of Christ and rearranged the tiles and stones to make the picture of an ugly dog. This is what the enemies of Truth have done to the word "love." It is as though they have taken Love itself, thrown a purple cloak on it to call it Lord and King, but then mocked it, fitted it with a crown of thorns, and beaten it senseless until it looked like the bruised and bloodied object they wanted it to be.

Just a few hours before Christ was arrested and beaten, He told His disciples that the world would recognize them when they love one another (John 13:35).

Jesus showed us what love looked like when He loved a sick and sinful world so much that He was willing to die for it. He showed men what love looked like when He loved His unfaithful bride so much that He was willing to die for her.

Years after Christ rose from the dead, the disciple whom He loved wrote that the love of God is that we keep His commandments. We may bristle at this, fearing that we are walking a tight-rope toward the false religion of salvation by works. But we know that we are only ever saved by Faith in Christ. With Christ's own righteousness accounted to us, we learn how to love, and by loving others we become the icons of Christ to both the believing and the unbelieving world. These commandments – that is to say, loving others – are not burdensome.

O Heavenly Father – You loved the world in such a way that You sent Your only Son to die, and promised that whoever believes in Him would not perish but have eternal life. Teach us to be thankful for the love You have shown us in Jesus Christ, and stir up in us the same love for others, that we may learn to remove the weeds and thorns from our hearts, and cultivate a life of virtuous love. Through the same Jesus Christ, Thy Son, our Lord. Amen.

Exorcism of the Mute Demon (Luke 11)

Third Sunday in Lent
Luke 11:14–28

"When a strong man, fully armed, guards his own palace, his goods are safe; but when one stronger than he attacks him and overcomes him, he takes away his armor in which he trusted and divides his spoil." (Luke 11:21–22, ESV)

God Himself Punished Christ

Without a doubt the Lord Jesus has redeemed us from sin, death, and the power of the devil by His holy, precious blood and innocent suffering and death. Through the Means of Grace, He continues to deliver poor sinners from the kingdom of the devil and bring them to live under Him in His kingdom forever. Christ is the Stronger Man who has attacked and overcome the strong man, the devil, to claim us as His own.

However, this does not mean that Christ paid our ransom to Satan. No, He paid the ransom to God. For it was God's perfect holiness and righteousness that demanded satisfaction for our sins and iniquities, and Christ truly made that satisfaction for the sins of the world by shedding His blood on the cross.

This week, our spiritual contemplation of Christ's suffering turns to the truth that God Himself was responsible for all that happened to Christ in His suffering. The arrest, scourging, crucifixion—all this came by God's own hand.

Note, however, that this is not just the Father's hand, for the perfect holiness and righteousness of the Father and of the Son and of the Holy Spirit is one. It is not wrong therefore to say that Christ rendered this satisfaction to Himself. Behold the love of God, that the Son of God should take upon Himself our sin and willingly step before His own righteous judgment in our place!

"In Christ God was reconciling the world to Himself, not counting their trespasses against them…For our sake He made Him to be sin who knew no sin, so that in Him we might become the righteousness of God." (2 Corinthians 5:19, 21)

O God, it was Your perfect will that Christ should suffer and die for the sins of the world. Grant that we acknowledge both the severity of our sins and the depth of Your divine love. Amen.

Monday, Lent 3
Zechariah 13:1-9

" "Awake, O sword, against my shepherd, against the man who stands next to me," declares the LORD of hosts. "Strike the shepherd, and the sheep will be scattered; I will turn my hand against the little ones. In the whole land, declares the LORD, two thirds shall be cut off and perish, and one third shall be left alive. And I will put this third into the fire, and refine them as one refines silver, and test them as gold is tested. They will call upon my name, and I will answer them. I will say, 'They are my people'; and they will say, 'The LORD is my God.' "" (Zechariah 13:7–9, ESV)

Jesus quotes this passage from Zechariah on the night of His betrayal and says, "For it is written, 'I will strike the shepherd, and the sheep of the flock will be scattered.'" With these words Christ our Lord gives the divine and perfect interpretation of Zechariah's prophecy, that it was the LORD of Hosts who struck His Good Shepherd. It was His sword that was awakened against the Son of Man who stands at the Father's right hand.

Why would the Lord God want to strike down His beloved Son? Zechariah declares: "They will call upon my name, and I will answer them. I will say, 'They are my people'; and they will say, 'The LORD is my God.'" It was not out of hatred for His Son but out of love for sinners that God willed to punish Jesus on the cross. Moreover, it was out of that same love for sinners that the Son was willing to take upon Himself the sins of His flock. Christ suffered God's wrath against our sin in order that we might become His people forever.

Because the Shepherd was struck down by God for the sins of the sheep, Christ has brought sinners from every nation under heaven into His fold to be God's people. Purchased by the blood of Christ, the redeemed members of the Shepherd's flock confess, "The LORD is my God."

O Christ, our Good Shepherd, we confess You to be our Lord and God, for You were willing to be struck down in order to make us Your people. Amen.

Tuesday, Lent 3
Acts 4:23-31

"for truly in this city there were gathered together against your holy servant Jesus, whom you anointed, both Herod and Pontius Pilate, along with the Gentiles and the peoples of Israel, to do whatever your hand and your plan had predestined to take place." (Acts 4:27–28, ESV)

In Revelation 13:8, the Apostle John writes of "the Lamb slain from the foundation of the world." (KJV) While it is certainly true that the sufferings and death of our Lord Jesus Christ took place at a definite time and at a definite place, it was the eternal will of God for Him to suffer and die, and His sufferings and death have eternal effects.

Indeed, from the first sin of Adam and Eve in the Garden of Eden, God spoke the promise of the Savior, the woman's Offspring, who would Himself suffer, His heel to be bruised by the serpent. God, in His perfect love and wisdom, kept that promise over the course of millennia through countless human agents, like Abraham, Isaac, Jacob, Judah, David, and many more.

Finally, in the fullness of time, the long-awaited Christ suffered and died at the hands of Herod and Pontius Pilate, along with the Gentiles and the peoples of Israel. Yet even with all of these human hands involved, going back to Adam and Eve in the beginning, it was always God's hand at work, doing what God's plan had predestined to take place.

To confess that God Himself was responsible for all that happened to Christ in His suffering is ultimately for our comfort. For nothing, not even His own suffering and death, was outside of Jesus' control. He testified, "No one takes [my life] from Me, but I lay it down of My own accord. I have authority to lay it down, and I have authority to take it up again. This charge I have received from My Father." (John 10:18) Though it was at the hands of both Jews and Gentiles alike, it was ultimately God's hand which struck down His Son, according to His eternal divine purpose for our everlasting salvation.

We praise You, O God, for You have loved us from eternity and so planned for our salvation from the foundation of the world. Amen.

Wednesday, Lent 3
Mark 14:26-50

"And he said, "Abba, Father, all things are possible for you. Remove this cup from me. Yet not what I will, but what you will."" *(Mark 14:36, ESV)*

One of the later heresies to arise in the early church about the Person of Christ is called "Monothelitism," which means, "one will." It falsely taught that, though our Lord Jesus Christ is indeed two natures, divine and human, He only possesses one will, that is, one ability to choose how to act.

The true doctrine, however, is that Jesus Christ is fully God and fully Man, truly human in every way: mind, body, soul, and will. If it were not so, then the Scriptures could not say that he "in every respect was tempted as we are." (Hebrews 4:15b) As Christ possesses two perfect natures, divine and human, so also he possesses two perfect wills, divine and human. Thus, Jesus confesses in John 6:38, "For I have come down from heaven, not to do My own will but the will of Him who sent Me."

Nevertheless, Jesus' human will is perfect and sinless. His human will was always in complete submission to God's will. Never once was Jesus' will opposed to the Father's will, but in every moment He could say, "My food is to do the will of Him who sent Me and to accomplish His work." (John 4:34)

This most certainly included His bitter sufferings and death. "It was the will of the LORD to crush Him," (Isaiah 53:10) so Jesus prayed in Gethsemane, "Yet not what I will, but You will." As in all things so also in His Passion our Lord Jesus gladly and willingly submitted to His Father's will. He became obedient unto death on the cross because He wanted to pay for our sins. Thus we rightly sing of Jesus, "He bears the stripes, the wounds, the lies, the mockery, and yet replies, 'All this I gladly suffer.'" (LSB 438:1)

Lord Jesus Christ, You gladly and willingly submitted to the Father's will and suffered death on the cross in order to pay for our sins. Grant us faith to submit to Your will in all things, for Your will is always best. Amen.

Thursday, Lent 3
Psalm 22

"For dogs encompass me; a company of evildoers encircles me; they have pierced my hands and feet— I can count all my bones— they stare and gloat over me; they divide my garments among them, and for my clothing they cast lots." (Psalm 22:16–18, ESV)

Psalm 22 is one of the clearest prophecies of the sufferings and death of our Lord Jesus Christ. Here David in the Spirit foretells the mockery endured by the Son of God, the piercing of His hands and feet by the nails, and the casting of lots for His garments by the soldiers. But above all is the first verse of this psalm, which Christ Himself prayed while hanging on the cross: "My God, My God, why have You forsaken Me?"

With these words we hear that Christ truly suffered and was in anguish because of God's wrath against sin. Indeed, it was God who poured out His wrath on the Son, as He had planned it from before the foundation of the world, and indeed the Son's will was perfectly in submission to the Father's will, so that He gladly suffered and died for us men and for our salvation. Nevertheless, the Lord Jesus Christ truly suffered all the physical agonies and torments of the scourging, the thorns, and the nails of the cross. By no means was He mimicking His suffering.

Even more than that, He truly suffered all the spiritual agonies of God's righteous wrath against sin. Bearing the sins of the world on the cross, Christ was accounted as the greatest sinner and treated as such, to the point of being forsaken by God.

Yet even in his torment, Jesus cried out, "My God." Yes, even in the darkest depths of woe, Jesus remained perfectly faithful, clinging to God and praying to Him as His own. By His perfect obedience, even in the hour of death, Christ has atoned for our disobedience, that we may live in God's presence forever.

Lord Jesus, You bore our sins and were forsaken by God, that we may dwell with You in heaven forever. Amen.

Friday, Lent 3
Job 13:1-28

"'Let me have silence, and I will speak, and let come on me what may. Why should I take my flesh in my teeth and put my life in my hand? Though he slay me, I will hope in him; yet I will argue my ways to his face. This will be my salvation, that the godless shall not come before him." (Job 13:13–16, ESV)

This week we have meditated on the sufferings and death of our Lord Jesus Christ, particularly contemplating the truth that it was God who poured out His wrath upon His Son. "It was the will of the LORD to crush him; He has put Him to grief." (Isaiah 53:10a)

Many years before Jesus' death, there was a blameless and upright man named Job, who feared God and turned away from evil. Yet God, in His mysterious wisdom, willed to afflict him severely, permitting Satan to take his possessions, his children, and his health from him. Despite all that he endured, Job remained faithful to God. Even in the depths of his suffering, Job confessed of God, "Though He slay me, I will hope in Him."

In the same way, even in the depths of His Passion, our Lord Jesus Christ remained faithful to His heavenly Father. As we heard yesterday, He still confessed God to be "My God," even while suffering the agonies of hell. When He took His final breath, He cried out, "Father, into Your hands I commit My spirit." (Luke 23:46)

Those who wait for the Lord shall never be put to shame. Job, after suffering, was restored and received from the Lord twice as much as he had before. Likewise, on the third day, God raised His Son from the dead, never to die again. Because He made Himself an offering for our guilt, the Lord Jesus has made us and many to be accounted righteousness for His sake. This was the Lord's will for Him; therefore we rejoice and are glad.

Heavenly Father, for us men and for our salvation You were willing to put Your Son to death. Grant us patience in our sufferings until we inherit eternal life by Your grace alone. Amen.

Saturday, Lent 3
John 8:1-11

"The scribes and the Pharisees brought a woman who had been caught in adultery, and placing her in the midst they said to him, "Teacher, this woman has been caught in the act of adultery. Now in the Law, Moses commanded us to stone such women. So what do you say?" This they said to test him, that they might have some charge to bring against him. Jesus bent down and wrote with his finger on the ground. And as they continued to ask him, he stood up and said to them, "Let him who is without sin among you be the first to throw a stone at her." And once more he bent down and wrote on the ground. But when they heard it, they went away one by one, beginning with the older ones, and Jesus was left alone with the woman standing before him." (John 8:3–9, ESV)

The Virtue of Justice

This curious episode in the life of Christ revolves around a woman caught in adultery. The scribes and Pharisees give the appearance of seeking justice for her crime against God, but in reality they only wanted to trip up Jesus. On some level, we must admit that it would have been just (that is to say, righteous) to stone this woman: the Bible clearly demanded it. Nonetheless, Jesus does not teach us that justice is bare obedience to the letter of the law with no regard to the spirit of the law. Jesus bends down and writes in the dirt, symbolizing that He is the one who wrote the Law in the first place, and that He is the ultimate authority on what it means to read, interpret, and enact the Law of the Old Testament.

Jesus bore the griefs and carried the sorrows of the woman caught in adultery. He knew that He would suffer for her infidelity when He was nailed to the cross, that He would feel the physical, emotional, and spiritual turmoil that her sin caused. This was the just decree of God: that the Son should die for the sins of the world.

We should not shy away from the just decrees of God, knowing that we are sinners, nor should we run from the just decree that calls us sons of God, righteous, regenerate, and little Christs. True justice is learned only from the words that Christ Himself wrote, cherish them for all they are worth.

Oh Jesus Christ, Your bride often sins against You, and we participate in that sin when we go chasing after other gods and man-made objects of our fear, love and trust. Teach us to humbly confess that the justice due to us for our sins is eternal damnation, and that the justice due to us on account of our faith in You is life everlasting. Stir us up that we would enact true justice in the world and spread Your righteousness by way of Your most holy word, for You live and reign with the Father and the Holy Ghost, ever one God, world without end. Amen.

Feeding the 5,000 (John 6)

Fourth Sunday in Lent
John 6:1-15

"Jesus said, "Have the people sit down." Now there was much grass in the place. So the men sat down, about five thousand in number." (John 6:10, ESV)

Christ's suffering as proof of God's love for us

Jesus feeds five thousand men (not counting women and children), multiplying five loaves of bread and two fish. In a desolate place, Jesus gives rest and refreshment to the large crowd that came to Him (v. 5). Halfway through the Lenten journey to Golgotha and Good Friday, it can seem like we're in a desolate place. The Lenten disciplines of fasting, prayer, and charity can begin to wear us down. It's a struggle. It's suffering from hunger pangs, from trying (and sometimes failing) to keep a regular time for prayer. It's sacrifice, giving to others as God has given to you, even when you don't want to be charitable.

Even amid struggle and suffering, Jesus gives hope, comfort, refreshment, and strength. Jesus doesn't just feed the rumbling bellies of five thousand households; He also heals their sick (Matthew 14:14) and teaches them (Mark 6:34; Luke 9:11). In that desolate place Jesus puts Philip to the test. Philip struggles to grapple with the issue at hand, but Jesus knew what He would do (John 6:6).

Are you struggling with the Lenten disciplines of fasting, prayer, and charity? Look to Jesus. Remember His fasting in the wilderness for forty days. Remember His fervent prayer in the Garden. Remember His charity to all who came to Him for mercy. He is your God and Lord. In Him alone, in His fasting and temptation, in His struggle and suffering and death do you find hope and strength.

The journey to Golgotha continues. Continue to hear the Word of God, the voice of Jesus. Be fed by Him at His altar. There He is charitable towards you. There He feeds you with the bread from heaven, His body and blood. He sets a table before you, a feast of rich food from heaven.

Sit in His holy presence. Every Christian household is given strength for the journey to see the face of God as His glory shines from the cross.

Lord Jesus, may Your Word be received by our minds, confessed with our lips, and treasured in our hearts. Amen.

Monday, Lent 4
Hosea 14:1-9

"Take with you words and return to the LORD; say to him, "Take away all iniquity; accept what is good, and we will pay with bulls the vows of our lips." (Hosea 14:2, ESV)

Confession is good for the soul, but absolution is even better. The Lord says through the prophet Hosea that the people are to, "Return, O Israel, to the LORD your God" (14:1). And on their lips is to be the words of their confession.

To confess is to echo back what God has already said in His Word. And what does God say about us? "Nothing good dwells in me" (Romans 7:18). We echo that, we repeat that, back to God that it is true. There is nothing good in me. I have turned away from the Lord my God. I have turned away from my neighbor in need. I have done what is evil in God's sight and transgressed His holy Law.

God places His Word into our ears so that we might repeat it back to Him. That's confession. We rightly confess, echo back, our sins. We have turned our face from God, He doesn't turn His face from His people. Instead, God turns His face from His only-begotten Son who carries the sins of the world (John 1:29; 2 Corinthians 5:21; Matthew 27:46). God turns His face away from Jesus who suffers in our place. His love for you is so high and so deep that He fulfills the Father's will taking your place and endures the wrath for all sin.

The Father turns His face towards you, He hears your confession, and for the sake of Christ, you are absolved. He takes away your iniquity and clothes you with the righteousness of Jesus. No sheep or bulls are required but only faith that sees the suffering love of Christ and says, "Amen!"

You might even say that it's dangerous to go alone. Take with you words and return to the LORD.

Jesus, Lamb of God, who takes away the sins of the world, open our lips and our mouths will declare your praise. Amen.

Tuesday, Lent 4
1 John 4:7-21

"In this is love, not that we have loved God but that he loved us and sent his Son to be the propitiation for our sins." (1 John 4:10, ESV)

When you see a cross, you're looking at an instrument of capital punishment. Used brutally by the Romans, a cross was the most humiliating and degrading form of execution. Yet this is how God shows His great love for the world. The only-begotten Son of God, born of a Virgin and laid in a manger, would stretch out His arms on the cross to embrace the world.

It seems so foolish to human reason that God would do such a thing. St. Paul tells the Corinthians, "But God chose what is foolish in the world to shame the wise; God chose what is weak in the world to shame the strong" (1 Corinthians 1:27). How often does God work how we want or expect Him to operate?

Yet this is His love that Jesus would be the propitiation for our sins. That He would be our covering, clothing over the shame of sin. Jesus tells the parable of the Pharisee and the tax collector in Luke 18. There the tax collector was "standing far off, would not even lift up his eyes to heaven, but beat his breast, saying, 'God, be merciful to me, a sinner'" (18:13). The word for "be merciful" is the same word used in 1 John 4:10 for propitiate.

The tax collector is saying, "God, cover me with Your righteousness for I am a sinner." In His love, God does cover you with the righteousness of Jesus. He suffers the pains of the cross and endures the shame for you. That's the love that the Father has for you, and He covers all your sins with the blood of Jesus. The cross isn't a tool for execution any longer, God turned it into the symbol of salvation and everlasting life – your salvation and eternal life.

God, cover us with Your righteousness for we are sinners. Lift up our eyes to the hill of Calvary for from there does our help come. Amen.

Wednesday, Lent 4
John 15:1-17

"Greater love has no one than this, that someone lay down his life for his friends." (John 15:13, ESV)

How many close friends do you have? Experts say that most people have about five close friends at a time because that's about the limit to what it takes to maintain those relationships. In the digital age, we can have hundreds or even thousands of "friends" on social media, many of whom we've never met in person. Favorite movies or TV shows can become so familiar that even the characters become a sort of "friend." Maybe that's why reboots of old shows are so popular for streaming services. But are they real friends?

There's a lack of genuine friendships in the digital age. Flesh and blood, real-life friendships between two people are rare. Sociologists and therapists can argue over the reasons for it and the solutions to it, but Scripture already gives a reason and a solution. Sin has separated us from the Lord, our maker and redeemer. Sin has also separated us from each other and turned us away from each other. This plays itself out in everyday life. Parents, children, coworkers, classmates, neighbors, even whole communities experience strife and hardships. Even individuals can experience inner hardships, strife, and struggles within their own selves. Mental health, anxiety, depression, stress, and how we deal with these are affected. We search for what's comfortable or what's familiar within ourselves to cope and ignore the flesh and blood people around us, even our brothers and sisters in the faith.

Jesus knows those struggles and hardships. He knows them better than you do. He's your flesh and blood friend that will never fail you. He calls you "Friend" and He lays down His life for you. He suffers in your stead. He endures the wrath for sin. He conquers, He triumphs, He wins the victory. His love for you, His friend, takes Him to the cross.

What language shall I borrow to thank Thee, dearest Friend, For this Thy dying sorrow, Thy pity without end? O make me Thine forever! And should I fainting be, Lord, let me never, never, Outlive my love for Thee. Amen. (LSB 449:3).

Thursday, Lent 4
Psalm 85

*"Show us your steadfast love, O L*ORD*, and grant us your salvation." (Psalm 85:7, ESV)*

"Pictures! Or it didn't happen!" We all want proof, photographic evidence that something happened. But with the onslaught of artificial intelligence infiltrating all parts of daily life, even pictures are suspect. Has it been altered? Was it created by AI? We want to be shown the evidence. Even before everyone had cell phone cameras in their pockets, the Psalmist cries out to God, "Show us your steadfast love, O LORD!" Show me that you love me, Lord!

That cry for evidence is answered by God on many occasions in Holy Scripture. By mighty deeds (Deuteronomy 26:8) God saved His people from slavery in Egypt. The disciples on the road to Emmaus saw it too, even though at that moment didn't believe or understand it (Luke 24:19).

Luther paints an amazing picture for us in his Easter hymn, "Christ Jesus Lay in Death's Strong Bands" (LSB 458) that shows the love of God as He saves us from slavery to sin and death:

> Here is the true Paschal Lamb
> Which God himself attested.
> That was on the tree of shame
> <u>In flaming passion roasted</u>
> His blood on our doorpost lies;
> Faith holds that before Death's eyes;
> The smiting angel can do naught. (Luther's Works v. 53:257)

What a vivid picture of Jesus enduring the Father's flaming wrath for sins. The Passover Lamb of God who takes away the sins of the world is roasted on the cross (Exodus 12:9) so strong His love to save us. Is there a greater way for God to show us His love and salvation? He provides the Lamb for a burnt offering (Genesis 22:8).

Jesus is the Passover Lamb whom God provided and shows His steadfast love. From the manger in Bethlehem to the cross at Calvary, you're shown the love of God and your salvation. "How greatly God must love thee" (LSB 372:4)!

Lord God, You show Your divine love at the cross as You provided the Lamb for the burnt offering. Grant that we may look upon Him in faith and be saved by Your grace alone. Amen.

Friday, Lent 4
Mark 14:32-42

"And he said to them, "My soul is very sorrowful, even to death. Remain here and watch."" (Mark 14:34, ESV)

The journey to Calvary continues, another week closer. The whole Church continues to watch as she hears these events of our Lord unfold before our ears once again. You hear of Jesus' sorrow and suffering. You hear Him say, *"My soul is very sorrowful, even to death."* Already, in the garden, Jesus is in sorrow. His final act of salvation, the hour has come. Jesus proves the Father's love for us in His sorrow and suffering. Jesus prays, "Remove this cup from me. Yet not what I will, but what you will" (Mark 14:36). Even in sorrow He obeys the Father's will. Jesus says to Peter, "Shall I not drink the cup that the Father has given me" (John 18:11)?

What cup shall Jesus drink? Psalm 75:8 reads: "For in the hand of the LORD there is a cup with foaming wine, well mixed, and he pours out from it, and all the wicked of the earth shall drain it down to the dregs." That's the cup He will drink in obedience to the Father, the cup of wrath. Instead of the wicked, the sinners, of the earth being left to drink it, Jesus drinks it down completely (to the dregs!).

The writer to the Hebrews says, "In the days of his flesh, Jesus offered up prayers and supplications, with loud cries and tears, to him who was able to save him from death, and he was heard because of his reverence" (Hebrews 5:7). There was no other way but through suffering, blood, and death. As Adam ate and sin came into the world in the Garden of Eden, the second Adam goes from the Garden of Gethsemane to suffer and die and by His sacrifice there is life for eternity for those who hear and believe.

We continue to watch and pray, knowing the cross and the empty tomb lay ahead of us. There will be hardship. There will be sorrow. There will be suffering. In the end, there is resurrection, life, and salvation.

Lord Jesus, in Your suffering You prove Your love for me and all people. Grant me steadfastness and courage that I may always watch and continue in prayer. Amen.

Saturday, Lent 4
John 8:12-30

"I am the one who bears witness about myself, and the Father who sent me bears witness about me." They said to him therefore, "Where is your Father?" Jesus answered, "You know neither me nor my Father. If you knew me, you would know my Father also." These words he spoke in the treasury, as he taught in the temple; but no one arrested him, because his hour had not yet come." (John 8:18–20, ESV)

The Virtue of Faith

Pious Christians usually don't find it particularly profound when they hear that Jesus is the perfect embodiment of something good. He is the perfection of obedience to earthly parents, He is the perfection of justice, prudence, courage, and love. But when we say that Christ is the perfect example of faith, we should pause and ask what that means. Scripture says that faith is "the conviction of things not seen," (Hebrews 11:1). But Jesus was the Word who has been since the beginning and He Himself has seen God. How, then, can He have faith?

When we look to Jesus as an example of virtuous living, we should not focus on His Divine Nature, but on His Human Nature. Christ, being fully man, was still bound by the law: this is why He was circumcised, why He kept the festivals, why He prayed, why He observed the Sabbath in its truest sense. So too, faith is and always has been the only way for man to access God's righteousness. Jesus Christ, born of the Virgin Mary, was still bound by this reality: He had to have faith in His Father.

It is for this reason that He chides the Jews who reject Him and thus reject His Father. True faith is complete trust in the power of the Trinity to create, preserve, save, and destroy. There is no such thing as believing in the Father without believing in the Son.

Thus, while we are called to faith in Christ Jesus, we participate in the same faith and we chase after the same faith that the Son had in the Father.

Oh Son of God, born of the Virgin to teach us men how to live: give us true faith that we may trust in You, Your Father, and the Holy Spirit who live and reign as one perfect Triune God. Amen.

Jesus threatened with stoning (John 8)

Fifth Sunday in Lent
John 8:46-59

"The Jews answered him, "Are we not right in saying that you are a Samaritan and have a demon?" Jesus answered, "I do not have a demon, but I honor my Father, and you dishonor me." (John 8:48–49, ESV)

As Christ suffered, so shall we

Christ provides a pattern for us today. The Jews slandered Christ. They slandered Him in two ways. They first slandered Him in His person. They called Him a Samaritan, a half-breed. They claimed He was no true Israelite at all, but a Pretender. Next, they slandered His office. They said He had a demon. They didn't say Jesus was possessed. They were saying that Jesus preached the doctrine of demons. No one could convict Jesus of sin, and yet they broke the Eighth Commandment by insulting Jesus' Person and His Teaching.

But look at Christ's response. He doesn't respond to the insult of His person. He doesn't respond for two reasons. First, He came to save the Samaritans and to preach to them, as He did in John chapter 4. Second, Christ didn't come to defend His own Person. That's not His goal. Jesus came to honor God the Father. He fulfills the First and Second Commandment. Jesus does not care about His own reputation but defends and exalts His Father in heaven. This is why He says He does not have a demon. If Jesus didn't dispute that charge, He would not have been honoring His Father, Who gave Him the doctrine which He was to preach.

How shall we follow our Lord's example? First, let us not take insults to our person personally. The focus should not be on ourselves, but on honoring Christ and our Father in heaven. Let us put away all pride and self-love. Second, let us honor our Father. We honor our Father by speaking God's Word in its truth and purity and by living holy lives according to it. Help us to do this, dear Father in heaven!

Heavenly Father, help us to honor You as Christ did by speaking Your Word in its purity and by living holy lives according to it. Amen.

Monday, Lent 5
Job 1:6-22

"In all this Job did not sin or charge God with wrong." (Job 1:22, ESV)

There are two types of temptation. There are temptations to evil. These temptations are from Satan. The goal of the temptation to evil is to destroy us. The second type of temptation is the temptation to good. This temptation comes from God. The goal of this temptation is to test and strengthen our faith. In Job, we see both temptations. The devil seeks to destroy Job. God seeks to prove that Job is blameless and upright, who fears God and turns away from evil.

Job did not commit a particular sin. This is the theological problem of Job's friends. While seeking to comfort him, they end up accusing Job of committing some heinous sin. No, Job was tempted because no one was like him in all the earth. He was blameless and upright. He believed in our Savior God. And Job passed the test. He did not sin or charge God with wrong.

There was no one on earth like Jesus, Who was blameless and upright. He too was tempted. The devil tempted Christ to sin by coming off the cross. God the Father also tempted Christ to good. His temptation was not to strengthen faith, but to save us who believe from sin, death, and the devil. Even as He was forsaken by His Father, Jesus trusted in the Father. He did not sin nor charge God with wrong.

What shall we learn from the temptation of Job and Jesus? First, the innocent suffer temptation. Job was relatively innocent in that he had not committed a particular sin for punishment. He was tempted because he was righteous by faith. Jesus was innocent in an absolute sense. He committed no sin. Both suffered temptation. Therefore, we should expect temptation and not, like Job's friends, torture ourselves by obsessively looking for particular, heinous sins. Second, we should not sin or charge God with wrong in temptation. This temptation is for our good, because God either allows it or sends it to strengthen us.

Heavenly Father, You tested both Job and Christ with temptation. Although we are assailed by it, defend us and give us the victory over it. Amen.

Tuesday, Lent 5
1 Peter 4:12-19

"But rejoice insofar as you share Christ's sufferings, that you may also rejoice and be glad when his glory is revealed." (1 Peter 4:13, ESV)

Yesterday, we talked about temptation. Job lost his family and his possessions due to seemingly natural events and calamities. Today, we learn about particular suffering. Peter speaks of suffering due to our speech and conduct as Christians.

Suffering is viewed as evil. This is wrong. Suffering is good. Suffering is good for those who suffer for their crimes. To suffer as a murderer or evildoer is a good thing. It is a fit punishment for such evil and it keeps others from committing similar sins. Hopefully, such suffering will lead to repentance and to eternal life, as it did for the thief upon the cross. The suffering of evil doers is good. We know this. So many movies and books speak of malefactors getting their comeuppance. We like that.

But suffering is good even when a Christian suffers for their godly conduct. When we suffer for doing good, we share in Christ's sufferings. What a privilege! We don't deserve to share in Christ's sufferings. We are not perfect or holy. And yet, we are privileged or counted worthy of suffering for Christ and for sharing in His sufferings. This privilege is given to us by grace, God's unmerited favor.

If we share in Christ's sufferings, we ought to rejoice. Suffering is a good thing because it means that God loves us. It means that the Holy Spirit rests on you. It means that you are blessed. If you share in His sufferings, you shall also share in His glory when He is revealed from heaven on the last day to judge both the living and the dead.

Suffering is not a bad or evil thing. Suffering is good, whether you are a malefactor or a benefactor. Christ suffered as a Benefactor, a do-gooder, and was exalted to the right hand of God. May we share in His sufferings as benefactors so that we might share in His glory by grace when He is revealed.

Dear Jesus, help us to entrust our souls to You when we suffer evil according to Your will. Amen.

Wednesday, Lent 5
John 15:18-16:4

"'I have said all these things to you to keep you from falling away." (John 16:1, ESV)

Don't be surprised. Don't be scandalized when the world hates you. Don't forsake the Christian faith when you are persecuted. This is not surprising. Our Lord Jesus warned us. He told us of the pagan world and the godless culture of death with which we are surrounded. This world is not neutral. It hates Jesus. It hates the Father. It hates you.

Don't be surprised. Don't be scandalized when churches hate you. Don't fall away when you are persecuted by popes and Synodical officials. Jesus also warned us of those who looked godly and dwell in the church, the gathering, the synagogue. They will excommunicate us unjustly. They will even think that killing us is worship, liturgy, a service to God Himself.

Liberals and legalists will always find common cause against Christ and His church. As Jesus says: *"But the word that is written in their Law must be fulfilled: 'They hated me without a cause.'"* Do not be surprised. Do not fall away. Christ tells us you these things because He loves you. He doesn't want you to fall away because there are weeds in the field of the church. He doesn't want you to walk away from Him because you will face suffering at the hands of heathen evil doers. He doesn't want you to be scandalized when you suffer for doing what is right and holy and according to the Ten Commandments. We are not greater than our Master, Jesus. If He suffered, we too shall suffer.

Remember these words so that you are not surprised. Memorize these words so that you are not scandalized. Speak these words sitting at the table and at bedtime, so that our children might joyously take their stand on the arena's bloody sand. We have been chosen out of the world. We are blessed beyond measure. Read this Scripture so that the Helper, the Holy Spirit, may ever bring these words and warnings of Jesus into your mind and heart.

O Holy Spirit, Helper of all God's children, bring all Christ's warnings into our remembrance so that we are not scandalized in the hour of testing. Amen.

Thursday, Lent 5
Psalm 119:65-72

"It is good for me that I was afflicted, that I might learn your statutes." (Psalm 119:71, ESV)

Psalm 119 is the Christian's A B Cs of the praise, love, power, and use of God's Word. It is a little, condensed Bible, which gives great comfort to us Christians as we memorize and repeat it. God is good and He does good to us, especially in sending us His dear Son. This is why He teaches us His statutes, not only His laws but also His gracious decrees. He loves us and that is why He wants us not only to be obedient in the Law of God, but also to be comforted by God's gracious decree concerning Christ.

We know that we must become theologians or God-talkers. To be a theologian is to be a Christian. To rightly talk about God honors God's name. That's what we learn in the Second Commandment and in the First Petition of the Lord's Prayer. How shall we become theologians? First, we must pray that the Holy Spirit would enlighten our hearts to rightly understand and truly believe His word. Second, we meditate upon His Word. We think about the Word read and preached, ponder it, and treasure it in our hearts like Mary.

The final way in which we become theologians is through affliction. Affliction teaches us to dig deep into God's Word. Without affliction, we would never learn God's Word. We would be like the enthusiasts, who speculate concerning God's Word.

It is good for us to be afflicted. Jesus Himself was afflicted. Hebrews 5:8 says that Jesus "learned obedience through what he suffered." If Jesus, the eternal and perfect Son of God learned obedience according to His human nature, then we too ought to walk in His steps. It is good when we are afflicted. Through affliction, we learn obedience to God's statues, just as Christ did.

Heavenly Father, Your Son learned obedience through suffering. Send this good affliction among us, that we might learn Your statutes and treasure Your Holy Word above all earthly riches. Amen.

Friday, Lent 5
Luke 23:44-47

"Then Jesus, calling out with a loud voice, said, "Father, into your hands I commit my spirit!" And having said this he breathed his last." (Luke 23:46, ESV)

Jesus has, by His perfect actions, taught us how to live. Now, Jesus teaches us how to die. According to every observation, Jesus' death was not blessed but terrible. He was hated, reviled, and wrongly convicted. He was shamed, robbed, and in intense pain. But that was nothing compared to what we see Godward. Jesus was accursed by God for hanging on a tree (Deut. 21:23). He was forsaken by His Father. He tasted death to its fullest.

And yet, despite all of this, Christ kept faith. He ran the race and prevailed in the fight. He, though rejected and scorned, commended His spirit into the hands of His Father. He never lost His trust in His Father. He knew, despite all observations to the contrary, that He was loved by God and had done all things well. He fully trusted that God would not leave His soul in hell, nor let His Christ see corruption.

One day, we too shall face death. We may suffer terribly in body. We may be afflicted in our souls with doubts and the devil's accusations. According to every observation, the world may think that we died a terrible death. But that's not true. Let us commend our spirits into the hand of our Savior God, Who redeems us from every sin and takes us to Himself in heaven. Let us not stumble at the finish line, but boldly and joyous finish the race, trusting that Jesus has gone ahead of us to prepare a place for us in His Father's mansions.

Everything may look like God is against us. But He is not. God is for you. God is for you because of Jesus. God, even as He forsook Christ, still loved Christ and knew Him to be His beloved Son. You are the Father's beloved son by faith. Learn from Jesus how to die.

Heavenly Father, Our Lord Jesus commended His spirit into Your hands. Give us the faith and the courage to commend ourselves daily and in death into Your gracious hands. Amen.

Saturday, Lent 5
1 Corinthians 6:9-14

""All things are lawful for me," but not all things are helpful. "All things are lawful for me," but I will not be dominated by anything. "Food is meant for the stomach and the stomach for food"—and God will destroy both one and the other. The body is not meant for sexual immorality, but for the Lord, and the Lord for the body." (1 Corinthians 6:12–13, ESV)

The Virtue of Temperance

All things are lawful to the Christian, but not all things are beneficial. We are about to enter into Holy Week, so let us re-up our Lenten discipline and teach our body to refrain from too much food, to flee from sexual immorality, and to chase after the temperance shown by our Lord Jesus Christ.

Even on the night He was betrayed, Jesus said He would not drink wine until He drank it anew in His father's kingdom – wine which gladdens the heart would no longer be on the tongue of the God who planted the grapes. The bread, which He broke, would not be given to him for sustenance while He was being taken from the Sanhedrin to Pilate to Herod.

Unlike Prudence – which is a call to discern the good from the evil – temperance is a more mature virtue that can recognize something as "good" but still refrain from indulging in it. This virtue is also sometimes called self-control, moderation, or sound-mindedness. It is only after the season of Lent, by practicing the other virtues and Christian disciplines, that we can begin to see Temperance grow in our bodies and minds.

Thus, when Christians abstain from meat or strong drink, or when married couples abstain from the marriage bed, it is a way of demonstrating the same temperance that our Lord did throughout His life, but especially during the days leading up to His crucifixion.

As we learn to crucify our desires – even our Godly desires – we will learn to live a life of patience and love toward others. May we who have denied ourselves this Lenten season, be found worthy to enter into the feast of Easter.

O Jesus Christ, you are about to begin your slow ride to the Cross, humble and mounted on a donkey. Teach us to deny earthly comforts that we may learn to suffer with you, so that we may someday die with you, so that we may someday rise from the dead just as you did on that Easter day. To you be all Glory now and forever. Amen.

Triumphal Entry (Matthew 21)

Palm Sunday
Matthew 26:1-27:66

"When Jesus had finished all these sayings, he said to his disciples, "You know that after two days the Passover is coming, and the Son of Man will be delivered up to be crucified."" *(Matthew 26:1–2, ESV)*

Holy Week spiritual contemplations on Christ's suffering

The Gospel account on Palm Sunday recites the entire account of Christ's Passion. Whereas we hear the Triumphant Entry in the beginning of the divine service, it is not until the reading of the Gospel do we get to the point. With all the shouts of "hosanna," waving palm branches, and casting of cloaks for the king to walk on—our eyes must not be so distracted that we cannot see the reason for Christ's mission: "the Son of Man will be delivered up to be crucified."

Jesus came into Jerusalem, not as an earthly king or revolutionary teacher, but as God's sacrifice. Jesus came for you to die on a cross as a payment for the wrath God. Like every week before the divine service, we examine ourselves and we see nothing but sin. And yet, we have today—not just Palm Sunday, but every Sunday rolled into one, where Jesus comes to you in his Word. Jesus comes to you here, not on a donkey, but as your Lord and king, giving you His promise in the name that is placed on your heads, and feeding you the banquet feast of life everlasting—the forgiveness of sins.

The point of Palm Sunday is Jesus—coming to suffer for you and brining you salvation on the cross, where He will be glorified as your King. Jesus comes to you today. He will cast His arms across the beams ready to receive you and all sinners. On Palm Sunday, we receive Jesus as who He is: the humble Lamb of God, the sacrifice; the king and priest; the life and salvation; the Man sitting upon a donkey, riding for us, to redeem us—to forgive you.

Gracious Father, teach us ever to behold Your Son rightly so that our hearts may be kindled to a right faith in Him who takes away the sins of the world, Jesus Christ, our Lord. Amen.

Anointing of Jesus (John 12)

Holy Monday
John 12:1-43

"Mary therefore took a pound of expensive ointment made from pure nard, and anointed the feet of Jesus and wiped his feet with her hair. The house was filled with the fragrance of the perfume." (John 12:3, ESV)

The costly ointment, myrrh, that Mary pours upon Jesus and then wiping His feet with her hair is nothing short of sincere love and devotion she had towards Jesus. It was a welcomed and spontaneous act. Whatever cost and luxury this ointment signified meant nothing to Mary. No expense could have been spared for her love of Christ had so overwhelmed her that she could do nothing more than to adorn the object of her sincere faith.

Contrast this action with the false faith of Judas who rebukes her action with false humility and lying tongue as to suggest that the flask be sold, and the money given to the poor. This grievous man, seduced by the Devil, had already sought to find a means to consume this money for himself. Where sin lies deep, there faith cannot reside. There was neither sincere love of God nor neighbor. Neither fear of God nor man. Whereas Mary had acted with beauty, grace, and virtue towards her Christ, Judas was captivated by avarice and greed—even toward the same Christ.

Although Mary's actions truly prepared Jesus for His burial, it will be finally Judas who brings death to Jesus' face. Jesus did not stop Mary from her worshipful behaviors and nor did He stop Judas from completing his mission. This, too, our Lord suffered. That, not willing to expose the treachery that was sure to come, He warned that He too will be gone from Judas and the time was short to turn away from sin and repent. None the less, our Christ received both: the love of a beloved a child and the betraying kiss. Soon, from this day, the funeral preparations will be complete and the procession to the cross will commence.

Merciful Lord, through the example of Your servant, Mary, You have revealed a glimpse of proper worship towards our Savior. Embolden us to turn from our sinful desires and evermore hold Christ in our hearts as our greatest treasure. Through Jesus Christ, our Lord. Amen.

Jesus finds the disciples asleep (Mark 14)

Holy Tuesday
Mark 14:1-15:47

"Then Judas Iscariot, who was one of the twelve, went to the chief priests in order to betray him to them. And when they heard it, they were glad and promised to give him money. And he sought an opportunity to betray him." (Mark 14:10–11, ESV)

Judas did not cling to Jesus with his heart. Immediately hearing the uplifting of Mary's anointing gift and his reprimand, he went to the chief priests who sought to use the opportunity of this disgruntled disciple. Judas leagued with those who sought to kill Jesus. Jesus was condemned by these high priests, scribes, and elders. They wanted to appear pious but sought evil; they wanted to remain as the arbiters of churchly doctrine and practice, and they would stir up as much trouble as they could with the local authorities and crowds if it would stop, if not hinder, the work of Jesus. Christ and His teachings are alleged to be false, heretical, and blasphemous. The betrayers of God intended to end Jesus. But, what these short-sighted men could not fathom is that this entire matter was the Father's divine plan.

When we consider these actions against Christ, we must also remember that Christ had also permitted himself to be sentenced to death for confessing to be God's own beloved Son. It was these charges that brought Jesus before the High Council to be tried as a blasphemer. It was to these men Jesus remained mostly silent to the false accusations. He remained silent as a lamb as He was crowned with thorns and draped with a mocking kingly-garment. Yes, the Christ was betrayed by one of His own. But it was His greatest love that He would undergo the threats of the Devil's efforts so that He may conquer them because of our weaknesses. He let himself be accused so that He may atone even for your sins and theirs, Christ permitted Himself to be betrayed, stripped, and wounded.

Father of all mercies, You gave Your Son into the hands of evil men so that He may bring to the completion Your divine plan of reconciliation. Create in us pure hearts that would seek forgiveness for our sins and recognize the love of our Savior. Amen.

Judas agrees to betray Jesus (Luke 22)

Holy Wednesday
Luke 22:1 - Luke 23:56

"And being in agony he prayed more earnestly; and his sweat became like great drops of blood falling down to the ground." (Luke 22:44, ESV)

This event takes place after eating and supping in the comfort of the upper room where Christ gave to His disciples His true body in bread and true blood in wine. We find Jesus traversing the garden with His remaining disciples to a place of darkness and solitude. It is Christ who goes to His place of anguish to pray to His Father and leaves only the admonition that His friends pray so that the Devil's marshaling forces would not lead them into temptation, shame, and vice. This prayer Christ still prays for us.

But this is the mere reality of it all. Death came for our Lord. It is the plain fact that the entire weight of the sins of the world were cast upon His shoulders that led Christ to beg that this cup would pass from Him. The weight of the cross began to weigh heavy even before the nails, beams, and hammers. God laid all our sins upon Him and Christ became so terribly distressed that the first drops of His innocent blood was mixed with His sweat from His brow. His Father who took Him from His heavenly throne placed Him as a man on this earth so that He would press to this exact moment in the vale of tears to drink the cup of wrath that was meant for His brothers. Jesus is an obedient Son. He took the cup and carried out the will of God. He gave Himself up to be killed so that we might He might release us from our enslavement to the Devil and death. This is God's will, so it is also Christ's will. He wanted to pay for our sin. Thus, He took the cup and drank the wrathful pour and emptied the dram.

Gracious God, Your Son prayed in the Garden that Your will be done on earth as it is heaven, even the forgiveness of sins. May the blood that Your Son shed for us continue to fill our cup with the blessings of faith to see Him as our Lord and Savior. Amen.

The Lord's Supper from a 1558 Book of Luther's Sermons

Maundy Thursday
John 13:1-15

"Jesus, knowing that the Father had given all things into his hands, and that he had come from God and was going back to God, rose from supper. He laid aside his outer garments, and taking a towel, tied it around his waist. Then he poured water into a basin and began to wash the disciples' feet and to wipe them with the towel that was wrapped around him." (John 13:3–5, ESV)

The Lord knew that His hour had come and the time to fulfill all things was at hand. His love drove Him through all suffering and agony. His love is His nature and is always outpouring toward the weak and sinning children. This is the position that Jesus takes when He washes His disciples feet: a place of divine humility and sincere love.

It was out of love that God sent His son to die for you. It is because Christ loved you that He gave Himself up for you. When we look upon the entire story of the Passion we should see that all that Christ had suffered for you should show His tremendous love towards you. It His love that makes us clean. And your feet were dirty with the dried mud stains of sin. Jesus washed them with His water, He washed them with His blood, and He washed them with the blood, sweat, and tears of His crucifixion.

On this Maundy Thursday we receive another testament of His love. Look up from your feet and pay attention to Holy Supper. Look at the cross which looms over the elements. Look at the sacrificial love in His true body in the cup of bread and the blood pouring into the chalice and flagon. As Christians we should seek after Christ's love and His supper with ravenous hunger. So that by doing so our bold confession of Christ will only join the unified church saying: "this is Christ, the son of God!"

O God, Your Son poured out His love for us on the cross as payment for our sins and satisfaction for our unrighteousness. He also gave us this Holy Meal as a testament of His love and fidelity to us and the forgiveness of sins. Give us grace in this sacrament that we may always love You and seek from You all good things. Amen.

The Crucifixion of Jesus By Lucas Cranach the Elder

Good Friday
John 18:1-John 19:42

"After this, Jesus, knowing that all was now finished, said (to fulfill the Scripture), "I thirst." A jar full of sour wine stood there, so they put a sponge full of the sour wine on a hyssop branch and held it to his mouth. When Jesus had received the sour wine, he said, "It is finished," and he bowed his head and gave up his spirit." (John 19:28–30, ESV)

The fact that Jesus took upon your sins means that He is your substitute. The righteous and innocent Man had to tremble and fear like a poor, condemned sinner and submitted to God's wrath. Just as the Scriptures also say, "Christ redeemed us from the curse of the law by becoming a curse for us—cursed is everyone who hangs on a tree (Gal 3)."

The work that Christ completed can never be exhausted. Christ released us from our sins, from the world, and even Satan. He went to the cross to suffer in our place what we deserved from God's judgement. Christ although sinless, was condemned to that we might be absolved. Christ bore the crown of death's thorns so that He could win for us the crown of life. Christ undertook the curse of God's forsakenness so that we would be remembered by God in love. It has even been said, in better words elsewhere, that Christ's last taste of earthly beverage, vinegar from a branch, He drank because He so thirsted for your salvation.

This Jesus Christ had patiently suffered all the cruelties that were thrust upon Him. Then, having after all the great prophecies being completed, after all Jesus agonized and endured, even accomplishing everything that belonged to God's plan of salvation, then Jesus announced: it is finished. The suffering is over. Death is done. Satan is defeated. God's wrath is satisfied. You are saved.

Lord God, heavenly Father, look in favor upon us Your children and forgive us all our sins and comfort us with the redemption won for us by the sacrifice of Your beloved Son Jesus Christ. By Your enduring love may our hope increase in the fullest confidence in Christ, the Lamb of God who takes away the sin of the world. Amen.

Crucifixion and Open Tomb

Holy Saturday
Mark 15:46-47

"And Joseph bought a linen shroud, and taking him down, wrapped him in the linen shroud and laid him in a tomb that had been cut out of the rock. And he rolled a stone against the entrance of the tomb. Mary Magdalene and Mary the mother of Joses saw where he was laid." (Mark 15:46–47, ESV)

The Virtue of Hope

What hope did the disciples have when they had watched their God die and then be placed in a tomb? What hope did the mother of Jesus have when she heard her Son commend her into the house of Saint John? What hope did Joseph of Arimathea have, save that Jesus would be given a fitting burial after His death?

In some ways, that first Holy Saturday saw a hopeless world. We know from the Scriptures that after Christ rose from the dead, many of his followers didn't believe it. This is because they had no hope. Or, to use the words of Christ, they were "foolish and slow to believe all that the prophets have spoken!" (Luke 24:25).

Jesus, however, never lost hope. He demonstrated that even in the midst of pain and suffering and anxiety that He could hope in the God who formed His body in the womb of the Virgin Mary. Though we may find ourselves with dwindling hope, we have a perfect example in Christ Jesus, who hoped that all things would work for the good of God – and His hope was perfectly fulfilled when His blood was shed for the sins of all time and space. Christ Jesus still hopes – since it is the Father alone who knows the day of His return – that there will be a day where there is no more hunger or thirst or pain or suffering, and when every tear is wiped away.

O God, our Heavenly Father, as the sun begins to set this evening, we can already hear the drums, the cymbals, and the lyres making a joyful noise to the God who defeats death. Though we are about to enter into the feast which knows no law, teach us in the coming days to strive after Prudence, Justice, Courage, and Temperance. Teach us to treasure in our hearts the faith You have given us, the Hope You have promised us, and above all the love that lasts into eternity. To You, O God, who raised Your Son from the Dead, who sent the Holy Spirit to guide the Church, be all glory now and forever. Amen.

The Empty Tomb

The Resurrection of our Lord - Easter Sunday
Mark 16:1-8

"And he said to them, "Do not be alarmed. You seek Jesus of Nazareth, who was crucified. He has risen; he is not here. See the place where they laid him." (Mark 16:6, ESV)

Christ is risen! He is risen indeed! Alleluia! The text says "who was crucified". This is what we have been contemplating this Lenten season. Jesus, who was crucified. That statement of the angel teaches us much we can think upon. As we have read, learned, and prayed this past season about Christ's suffering, we have done so knowing and believing that it indeed did happen just as Holy Scripture teaches us. It has happened. As we heard on Friday, it is finished.

His crucifixion will continue to have an effect, however. That's what the language tells us. It has been done. It has happened. History. The fruit of that one act of sacrifice continues to bear much fruit. It is because of Jesus who was crucified that we are baptized, washed clean in that washing of renewal and regeneration of the Holy Spirit. It is because of Jesus who was crucified that we continue to receive absolution for our sins. It is because of Jesus who was crucified that we can gather on days like today to receive the forgiveness of sins along with the Body and Blood of the Crucified One.

This finds its way into our lives as well. Because of the once, for all event of our Lord Jesus Christ's crucifixion that we can hear the Gospel over and over from our pastors, from our parents, from our brothers and sisters in the faith. The fruit of His crucifixion fills congregations, homes, schools, workplaces, and communities.

The resurrection of Jesus, that we gather to celebrate with feasts and festivities today is God's proof to all of us that Jesus, God's only begotten Son, was crucified, and that truly we do not need to be alarmed. Nothing can now separate us from God's love shown to us in Christ Jesus, who was crucified.

In that way, the crucifixion will bear fruit for us all in eternity. This is why our Easter texts can so emphasize the end of death. Jesus defeated it by dying. It has lost its sting. It is no longer our master. The proof is that Christ, who was crucified, is now and ever shall be living. Christ is risen! He is risen indeed! Alleluia!

Almighty God, the Father of our Lord Jesus Christ, today we give you praise and thanksgiving for raising Your Son from the dead, confirming that He who was crucified is now the source of all our lives. Keep us faithful unto the end. Amen.

Appendix

The Passion of Our Lord Jesus Christ Drawn from All Four Gospels

With permission from:

https://wolfmueller.co/the-passion-of-jesus-drawn-from-all-four-gospels/

Scripture taken from the New King James Version®. Copyright © 1982 by Thomas Nelson. Used by permission. All rights reserved.

Portions selected from Matthew 26:15-27:66, Mark 14:12-15:47, Luke 22:7-23:56, and John 13:1-19:42, arranged chronologically to tell the story of the arrest, trials, suffering, crucifixion, death, and burial of our Lord Jesus.

Events occur on Thursday and Friday, 13-14 Nissan (April 2-3), 33AD, in and around Jerusalem

1/ Preparation for the Passover
Into Jerusalem

LUKE 22:7 Then came the Day of Unleavened Bread, when the Passover must be killed. ⁸ And He sent Peter and John, saying, "Go and prepare the Passover for us, that we may eat."

⁹ So they said to Him, "Where do You want us to prepare?"

¹⁰ And He said to them, "Behold, when you have entered the city, a man will meet you carrying a pitcher of water; follow him into the house which he enters. ¹¹ Then you shall say to the master of the house, 'The Teacher says to you, "Where is the guest room where I may eat the Passover with My disciples?"' ¹² Then he will show you a large, furnished upper room; there make ready."

¹³ So they went and found it just as He had said to them, and they prepared the Passover.

2/ Washing the Disciples Feet
Jerusalem, Upper Room

JOHN 13:1 Now before the Feast of the Passover, when Jesus knew that His hour had come that He should depart from this world to the Father, having loved His own who were in the world, He loved them to the end.

² And supper being ended, the devil having already put it into the heart of Judas Iscariot, Simon's *son*, to betray Him, ³ Jesus, knowing that the Father had given all things into His hands, and that He had come from God and was

going to God, ⁴ rose from supper and laid aside His garments, took a towel and girded Himself. ⁵ After that, He poured water into a basin and began to wash the disciples' feet, and to wipe *them* with the towel with which He was girded. ⁶ Then He came to Simon Peter. And *Peter* said to Him, "Lord, are You washing my feet?"

⁷ Jesus answered and said to him, "What I am doing you do not understand now, but you will know after this."

⁸ Peter said to Him, "You shall never wash my feet!"

Jesus answered him, "If I do not wash you, you have no part with Me."

⁹ Simon Peter said to Him, "Lord, not my feet only, but also *my* hands and *my* head!"

¹⁰ Jesus said to him, "He who is bathed needs only to wash *his* feet, but is completely clean; and you are clean, but not all of you." ¹¹ For He knew who would betray Him; therefore He said, "You are not all clean."

¹² So when He had washed their feet, taken His garments, and sat down again, He said to them, "Do you know what I have done to you? ¹³ You call Me Teacher and Lord, and you say well, for *so* I am. ¹⁴ If I then, *your* Lord and Teacher, have washed your feet, you also ought to wash one another's feet. ¹⁵ For I have given you an example, that you should do as I have done to you. ¹⁶ Most assuredly, I say to you, a servant is not greater than his master; nor is he who is sent greater than he who sent him. ¹⁷ If you know these things, blessed are you if you do them.

¹⁸ "I do not speak concerning all of you. I know whom I have chosen; but that the Scripture may be fulfilled, '*He who eats* bread with Me has lifted up his heel against Me.' ¹⁹ Now I tell you before it comes, that when it does come to pass, you may believe that I am *He*. ²⁰ Most assuredly, I say to you, he who receives whomever I send receives Me; and he who receives Me receives Him who sent Me."

3/ The Lord's Supper

MATTHEW 26:20 When evening had come, He sat down with the twelve. ²¹ Now as they were eating, He said, "Assuredly, I say to you, one of you will betray Me."

²² And they were exceedingly sorrowful, and each of them began to say to Him, "Lord, is it I?"

²³ He answered and said, "He who dipped *his* hand with Me in the dish will betray Me. ²⁴ The Son of Man indeed goes just as it is written of Him, but woe to that man by whom the Son of Man is betrayed! It would have been good for that man if he had not been born."

²⁵ Then Judas, who was betraying Him, answered and said, "Rabbi, is it I?"

He said to him, "You have said it."

LUKE 22:14 When the hour had come, He sat down, and the twelve apostles with Him. ¹⁵ Then He said to them, "With *fervent* desire I have desired to eat this Passover with you before I suffer; ¹⁶ for I say to you, I will no longer eat of it until it is fulfilled in the kingdom of God."

¹⁷ Then He took the cup, and gave thanks, and said, "Take this and divide *it* among yourselves; ¹⁸ for I say to you, I will not drink of the fruit of the vine until the kingdom of God comes."

MATTHEW 26:26 And as they were eating, Jesus took bread, blessed and broke *it*, and gave *it* to the disciples and said, "Take, eat; this is My body."

²⁷ Then He took the cup, and gave thanks, and gave *it* to them, saying, "Drink from it, all of you. ²⁸ For this is My blood of the new covenant, which is shed for many for the remission of sins. ²⁹ But I say to you, I will not drink of this fruit of the vine from now on until that day when I drink it new with you in My Father's kingdom."

4/ Jesus Foretells His Betrayal

John 13:21 When Jesus had said these things, He was troubled in spirit, and testified and said, "Most assuredly, I say to you, one of you will betray Me." ²² Then the disciples looked at one another, perplexed about whom He spoke.

²³ Now there was leaning on Jesus' bosom one of His disciples, whom Jesus loved. ²⁴ Simon Peter therefore motioned to him to ask who it was of whom He spoke.

²⁵ Then, leaning back on Jesus' breast, he said to Him, "Lord, who is it?"

²⁶ Jesus answered, "It is he to whom I shall give a piece of bread when I have dipped *it*." And having dipped the bread, He gave *it* to Judas Iscariot, *the son* of Simon. ²⁷ Now after the piece of bread, Satan entered him. Then Jesus said to him, "What you do, do quickly." ²⁸ But no one at the table knew for what reason He said this to him. ²⁹ For some thought, because Judas had the money box, that Jesus had said to him, "Buy *those things* we need for the feast," or that he should give something to the poor.

³⁰ Having received the piece of bread, he then went out immediately. And it was night.

5/ Two Swords

LUKE 22:35 And He said to them, "When I sent you without money bag, knapsack, and sandals, did you lack anything?"

So they said, "Nothing."

³⁶ Then He said to them, "But now, he who has a money bag, let him take *it,* and likewise a knapsack; and he who has no sword, let him sell his garment

and buy one. ³⁷ For I say to you that this which is written must still be accomplished in Me: *'And He was numbered with the transgressors.'* For the things concerning Me have an end."

³⁸ So they said, "Lord, look, here *are* two swords."

And He said to them, "It is enough."

6/ Jesus Valedictory Speech, and High Priestly Prayer

JOHN 14:1 "Let not your heart be troubled; you believe in God, believe also in Me. ² In My Father's house are many mansions; if *it were* not *so,* I would have told you. I go to prepare a place for you. ³ And if I go and prepare a place for you, I will come again and receive you to Myself; that where I am, *there* you may be also. ⁴ And where I go you know, and the way you know."

⁵ Thomas said to Him, "Lord, we do not know where You are going, and how can we know the way?"

⁶ Jesus said to him, "I am the way, the truth, and the life. No one comes to the Father except through Me.

⁷ "If you had known Me, you would have known My Father also; and from now on you know Him and have seen Him."

⁸ Philip said to Him, "Lord, show us the Father, and it is sufficient for us."

⁹ Jesus said to him, "Have I been with you so long, and yet you have not known Me, Philip? He who has seen Me has seen the Father; so how can you say, 'Show us the Father'? ¹⁰ Do you not believe that I am in the Father, and the Father in Me? The words that I speak to you I do not speak on My own *authority;* but the Father who dwells in Me does the works. ¹¹ Believe Me that I *am* in the Father and the Father in Me, or else believe Me for the sake of the works themselves.

¹² "Most assuredly, I say to you, he who believes in Me, the works that I do he will do also; and greater *works* than these he will do, because I go to My Father. ¹³ And whatever you ask in My name, that I will do, that the Father may be glorified in the Son. ¹⁴ If you ask anything in My name, I will do *it.*

¹⁵ "If you love Me, keep My commandments. ¹⁶ And I will pray the Father, and He will give you another Helper, that He may abide with you forever— ¹⁷ the Spirit of truth, whom the world cannot receive, because it neither sees Him nor knows Him; but you know Him, for He dwells with you and will be in you. ¹⁸ I will not leave you orphans; I will come to you.

¹⁹ "A little while longer and the world will see Me no more, but you will see Me. Because I live, you will live also. ²⁰ At that day you will know that I *am* in My Father, and you in Me, and I in you. ²¹ He who has My commandments and keeps them, it is he who loves Me. And he who loves Me will be loved by My Father, and I will love him and manifest Myself to him."

²² Judas (not Iscariot) said to Him, "Lord, how is it that You will manifest Yourself to us, and not to the world?"

²³ Jesus answered and said to him, "If anyone loves Me, he will keep My word; and My Father will love him, and We will come to him and make Our home with him. ²⁴ He who does not love Me does not keep My words; and the word which you hear is not Mine but the Father's who sent Me.

²⁵ "These things I have spoken to you while being present with you. ²⁶ But the Helper, the Holy Spirit, whom the Father will send in My name, He will teach you all things, and bring to your remembrance all things that I said to you. ²⁷ Peace I leave with you, My peace I give to you; not as the world gives do I give to you. Let not your heart be troubled, neither let it be afraid. ²⁸ You have heard Me say to you, 'I am going away and coming *back* to you.' If you loved Me, you would rejoice because I said, 'I am going to the Father,' for My Father is greater than I.

²⁹ "And now I have told you before it comes, that when it does come to pass, you may believe. ³⁰ I will no longer talk much with you, for the ruler of this world is coming, and he has nothing in Me. ³¹ But that the world may know that I love the Father, and as the Father gave Me commandment, so I do. Arise, let us go from here.

7/ Jesus Warns of Further Desertion, Cries of Loyalty from the Disciples
Leaving Jerusalem to the East, thru the Kidron Valley and to the Garden of Gethsemane
MATTHEW 26:30 And when they had sung a hymn, they went out to the Mount of Olives.

³¹ Then Jesus said to them, "All of you will be made to stumble because of Me this night, for it is written:

'I will strike the Shepherd,
And the sheep of the flock will be scattered.'

³² But after I have been raised, I will go before you to Galilee." LUKE 22:31 And the Lord said, "Simon, Simon! Indeed, Satan has asked for you, that he may sift *you* as wheat. ³² But I have prayed for you, that your faith should not fail; and when you have returned to *Me,* strengthen your brethren."

MATTHEW 26:33 Peter answered and said to Him, "Even if all are made to stumble because of You, I will never be made to stumble."

³⁴ Jesus said to him, "Assuredly, I say to you that this night, before the rooster crows, you will deny Me three times."

³⁵ Peter said to Him, "Even if I have to die with You, I will not deny You!"

And so said all the disciples.

8/ Teaching on the Way to the Garden of Gethsemane

15:1 "I am the true vine, and My Father is the vinedresser. ² Every branch in Me that does not bear fruit He takes away; and every *branch* that bears fruit He prunes, that it may bear more fruit. ³ You are already clean because of the word which I have spoken to you. ⁴ Abide in Me, and I in you. As the branch cannot bear fruit of itself, unless it abides in the vine, neither can you, unless you abide in Me.

⁵ "I am the vine, you *are* the branches. He who abides in Me, and I in him, bears much fruit; for without Me you can do nothing. ⁶ If anyone does not abide in Me, he is cast out as a branch and is withered; and they gather them and throw *them* into the fire, and they are burned. ⁷ If you abide in Me, and My words abide in you, you will ask what you desire, and it shall be done for you. ⁸ By this My Father is glorified, that you bear much fruit; so you will be My disciples.

⁹ "As the Father loved Me, I also have loved you; abide in My love. ¹⁰ If you keep My commandments, you will abide in My love, just as I have kept My Father's commandments and abide in His love.

¹¹ "These things I have spoken to you, that My joy may remain in you, and *that* your joy may be full.

¹² This is My commandment, that you love one another as I have loved you.
¹³ Greater love has no one than this, than to lay down one's life for his friends.
¹⁴ You are My friends if you do whatever I command you. ¹⁵ No longer do I call you servants, for a servant does not know what his master is doing; but I have called you friends, for all things that I heard from My Father I have made known to you. ¹⁶ You did not choose Me, but I chose you and appointed you that you should go and bear fruit, and *that* your fruit should remain, that whatever you ask the Father in My name He may give you.
¹⁷ These things I command you, that you love one another.

¹⁸ "If the world hates you, you know that it hated Me before *it hated* you.
¹⁹ If you were of the world, the world would love its own. Yet because you are not of the world, but I chose you out of the world, therefore the world hates you. ²⁰ Remember the word that I said to you, 'A servant is not greater than his master.' If they persecuted Me, they will also persecute you. If they kept My word, they will keep yours also. ²¹ But all these things they will do to you for My name's sake, because they do not know Him who sent Me. ²² If I had not come and spoken to them, they would have no sin, but now they have no excuse for their sin. ²³ He who hates Me hates My Father also. ²⁴ If I had not done among them the works which no one else did, they would have no sin; but now they have seen and also hated both Me and My Father. ²⁵ But *this*

happened that the word might be fulfilled which is written in their law, 'They hated Me without a cause.'

²⁶ "But when the Helper comes, whom I shall send to you from the Father, the Spirit of truth who proceeds from the Father, He will testify of Me. ²⁷ And you also will bear witness, because you have been with Me from the beginning.

¹⁶:¹ "These things I have spoken to you, that you should not be made to stumble. ² They will put you out of the synagogues; yes, the time is coming that whoever kills you will think that he offers God service. ³ And these things they will do to you because they have not known the Father nor Me. ⁴ But these things I have told you, that when the time comes, you may remember that I told you of them.

"And these things I did not say to you at the beginning, because I was with you.

⁵ "But now I go away to Him who sent Me, and none of you asks Me, 'Where are You going?' ⁶ But because I have said these things to you, sorrow has filled your heart. ⁷ Nevertheless I tell you the truth. It is to your advantage that I go away; for if I do not go away, the Helper will not come to you; but if I depart, I will send Him to you. ⁸ And when He has come, He will convict the world of sin, and of righteousness, and of judgment: ⁹ of sin, because they do not believe in Me; ¹⁰ of righteousness, because I go to My Father and you see Me no more; ¹¹ of judgment, because the ruler of this world is judged.

¹² "I still have many things to say to you, but you cannot bear *them* now. ¹³ However, when He, the Spirit of truth, has come, He will guide you into all truth; for He will not speak on His own *authority*, but whatever He hears He will speak; and He will tell you things to come. ¹⁴ He will glorify Me, for He will take of what is Mine and declare *it* to you. ¹⁵ All things that the Father has are Mine. Therefore I said that He will take of Mine and declare *it* to you.

¹⁶ "A little while, and you will not see Me; and again a little while, and you will see Me, because I go to the Father."

¹⁷ Then *some* of His disciples said among themselves, "What is this that He says to us, 'A little while, and you will not see Me; and again a little while, and you will see Me'; and, 'because I go to the Father'?" ¹⁸ They said therefore, "What is this that He says, 'A little while'? We do not know what He is saying."

¹⁹ Now Jesus knew that they desired to ask Him, and He said to them, "Are you inquiring among yourselves about what I said, 'A little while, and you will not see Me; and again a little while, and you will see Me'? ²⁰ Most assuredly, I say to you that you will weep and lament, but the world will rejoice; and you will be sorrowful, but your sorrow will be turned into joy. ²¹ A

woman, when she is in labor, has sorrow because her hour has come; but as soon as she has given birth to the child, she no longer remembers the anguish, for joy that a human being has been born into the world. ²² Therefore you now have sorrow; but I will see you again and your heart will rejoice, and your joy no one will take from you.

²³ "And in that day you will ask Me nothing. Most assuredly, I say to you, whatever you ask the Father in My name He will give you. ²⁴ Until now you have asked nothing in My name. Ask, and you will receive, that your joy may be full.

²⁵ "These things I have spoken to you in figurative language; but the time is coming when I will no longer speak to you in figurative language, but I will tell you plainly about the Father. ²⁶ In that day you will ask in My name, and I do not say to you that I shall pray the Father for you; ²⁷ for the Father Himself loves you, because you have loved Me, and have believed that I came forth from God. ²⁸ I came forth from the Father and have come into the world. Again, I leave the world and go to the Father."

²⁹ His disciples said to Him, "See, now You are speaking plainly, and using no figure of speech! ³⁰ Now we are sure that You know all things, and have no need that anyone should question You. By this we believe that You came forth from God."

³¹ Jesus answered them, "Do you now believe? ³² Indeed the hour is coming, yes, has now come, that you will be scattered, each to his own, and will leave Me alone. And yet I am not alone, because the Father is with Me. ³³ These things I have spoken to you, that in Me you may have peace. In the world you will have tribulation; but be of good cheer, I have overcome the world."

¹⁷:¹Jesus spoke these words, lifted up His eyes to heaven, and said: "Father, the hour has come. Glorify Your Son, that Your Son also may glorify You, ² as You have given Him authority over all flesh, that He should give eternal life to as many as You have given Him. ³ And this is eternal life, that they may know You, the only true God, and Jesus Christ whom You have sent. ⁴ I have glorified You on the earth. I have finished the work which You have given Me to do. ⁵ And now, O Father, glorify Me together with Yourself, with the glory which I had with You before the world was.

⁶ "I have manifested Your name to the men whom You have given Me out of the world. They were Yours, You gave them to Me, and they have kept Your word. ⁷ Now they have known that all things which You have given Me are from You. ⁸ For I have given to them the words which You have given Me; and they have received *them,* and have known surely that I came forth from You; and they have believed that You sent Me.

⁹ "I pray for them. I do not pray for the world but for those whom You have given Me, for they are Yours. ¹⁰ And all Mine are Yours, and Yours are Mine, and I am glorified in them. ¹¹ Now I am no longer in the world, but these are in the world, and I come to You. Holy Father, keep through Your name those whom You have given Me, that they may be one as We *are*. ¹² While I was with them in the world, I kept them in Your name. Those whom You gave Me I have kept; and none of them is lost except the son of perdition, that the Scripture might be fulfilled. ¹³ But now I come to You, and these things I speak in the world, that they may have My joy fulfilled in themselves. ¹⁴ I have given them Your word; and the world has hated them because they are not of the world, just as I am not of the world. ¹⁵ I do not pray that You should take them out of the world, but that You should keep them from the evil one. ¹⁶ They are not of the world, just as I am not of the world. ¹⁷ Sanctify them by Your truth. Your word is truth. ¹⁸ As You sent Me into the world, I also have sent them into the world. ¹⁹ And for their sakes I sanctify Myself, that they also may be sanctified by the truth.

²⁰ "I do not pray for these alone, but also for those who will believe in Me through their word; ²¹ that they all may be one, as You, Father, *are* in Me, and I in You; that they also may be one in Us, that the world may believe that You sent Me. ²² And the glory which You gave Me I have given them, that they may be one just as We are one: ²³ I in them, and You in Me; that they may be made perfect in one, and that the world may know that You have sent Me, and have loved them as You have loved Me.

²⁴ "Father, I desire that they also whom You gave Me may be with Me where I am, that they may behold My glory which You have given Me; for You loved Me before the foundation of the world. ²⁵ O righteous Father! The world has not known You, but I have known You; and these have known that You sent Me. ²⁶ And I have declared to them Your name, and will declare *it*, that the love with which You loved Me may be in them, and I in them."

9/ Agony in the Garden of Gethsemane
Garden of Gethsemane, Mt Olives (outside Jerusalem)

MARK 14:32 Then they came to a place which was named Gethsemane; and He said to His disciples, "Sit here while I pray." ³³ And He took Peter, James, and John with Him, and He began to be troubled and deeply distressed. ³⁴ Then He said to them, "My soul is exceedingly sorrowful, *even* to death. Stay here and watch."

³⁵ He went a little farther, and fell on the ground, and prayed that if it were possible, the hour might pass from Him. ³⁶ And He said, "Abba, Father, all

things *are* possible for You. Take this cup away from Me; nevertheless, not what I will, but what You *will*."

LUKE 22:43 Then an angel appeared to Him from heaven, strengthening Him. ⁴⁴ And being in agony, He prayed more earnestly. Then His sweat became like great drops of blood falling down to the ground.

MARK 14:37 Then He came and found them sleeping, and said to Peter, "Simon, are you sleeping? Could you not watch one hour? ³⁸ Watch and pray, lest you enter into temptation. The spirit indeed *is* willing, but the flesh *is* weak."

³⁹ Again He went away and prayed, and spoke the same words. ⁴⁰ And when He returned, He found them asleep again, for their eyes were heavy; and they did not know what to answer Him.

⁴¹ Then He came the third time and said to them, "Are you still sleeping and resting? It is enough! The hour has come; behold, the Son of Man is being betrayed into the hands of sinners. ⁴² Rise, let us be going. See, My betrayer is at hand."

10/ Jesus Betrayed and Arrested

JOHN 18:1 When Jesus had spoken these words, He went out with His disciples over the Brook Kidron, where there was a garden, which He and His disciples entered. ² And Judas, who betrayed Him, also knew the place; for Jesus often met there with His disciples. ³ Then Judas, having received a detachment *of troops,* and officers from the chief priests and Pharisees, came there with lanterns, torches, and weapons.

MATTHEW 26:47 And while He was still speaking, behold, Judas, one of the twelve, with a great multitude with swords and clubs, came from the chief priests and elders of the people.

⁴⁸ Now His betrayer had given them a sign, saying, "Whomever I kiss, He is the One; seize Him." ⁴⁹ Immediately he went up to Jesus and said, "Greetings, Rabbi!" and kissed Him.

⁵⁰ But Jesus said to him, "Friend, why have you come?"

JOHN 18:4 Jesus therefore, knowing all things that would come upon Him, went forward and said to them, "Whom are you seeking?"

⁵ They answered Him, "Jesus of Nazareth."

Jesus said to them, "I am *He.*" And Judas, who betrayed Him, also stood with them. ⁶ Now when He said to them, "I am *He,*" they drew back and fell to the ground.

⁷ Then He asked them again, "Whom are you seeking?"

And they said, "Jesus of Nazareth."

⁸ Jesus answered, "I have told you that I am *He*. Therefore, if you seek Me, let these go their way," ⁹ that the saying might be fulfilled which He spoke, "Of those whom You gave Me I have lost none."

¹⁰ Then Simon Peter, having a sword, drew it and struck the high priest's servant, and cut off his right ear. The servant's name was Malchus.

¹¹ So Jesus said to Peter, "Put your sword into the sheath. Shall I not drink the cup which My Father has given Me?" ᴹᴬᵀᵀᴴᴱᵂ ²⁶:⁵²ᴮ "All who take the sword will perish by the sword. ⁵³ Or do you think that I cannot now pray to My Father, and He will provide Me with more than twelve legions of angels? ⁵⁴ How then could the Scriptures be fulfilled, that it must happen thus?"

⁵⁵ In that hour Jesus said to the multitudes, "Have you come out, as against a robber, with swords and clubs to take Me? I sat daily with you, teaching in the temple, and you did not seize Me. ⁵⁶ But all this was done that the Scriptures of the prophets might be fulfilled."

Then all the disciples forsook Him and fled.

ᴹᴬᴿᴷ ¹⁴:⁵¹ Now a certain young man followed Him, having a linen cloth thrown around *his* naked *body*. And the young men laid hold of him, ⁵² and he left the linen cloth and fled from them naked.

11/ First Trial: Examination by Annas
Jerusalem, Annas' House

ᴶᴼᴴᴺ ¹⁸:¹² Then the detachment *of troops* and the captain and the officers of the Jews arrested Jesus and bound Him. ¹³ And they led Him away to Annas first, for he was the father-in-law of Caiaphas who was high priest that year. ¹⁴ Now it was Caiaphas who advised the Jews that it was expedient that one man should die for the people.

ᴶᴼᴴᴺ ¹⁸:¹⁹ The high priest then asked Jesus about His disciples and His doctrine.

²⁰ Jesus answered him, "I spoke openly to the world. I always taught in synagogues and in the temple, where the Jews always meet, and in secret I have said nothing. ²¹ Why do you ask Me? Ask those who have heard Me what I said to them. Indeed they know what I said."

²² And when He had said these things, one of the officers who stood by struck Jesus with the palm of his hand, saying, "Do You answer the high priest like that?"

²³ Jesus answered him, "If I have spoken evil, bear witness of the evil; but if well, why do you strike Me?"

12/ Second Trial: Home of Caiaphas, High Priest (and the Betrayal of Peter)

Jerusalem, House of Caiaphas

JOHN 18:24 Then Annas sent Him bound to Caiaphas the high priest. MARK 14:53 And they led Jesus away to the high priest; and with him were assembled all the chief priests, the elders, and the scribes. 54 But Peter followed Him at a distance, right into the courtyard of the high priest. And he sat with the servants and warmed himself at the fire.

55 Now the chief priests and all the council sought testimony against Jesus to put Him to death, but found none. 56 For many bore false witness against Him, but their testimonies did not agree.

57 Then some rose up and bore false witness against Him, saying, 58 "We heard Him say, 'I will destroy this temple made with hands, and within three days I will build another made without hands.'" 59 But not even then did their testimony agree.

60 And the high priest stood up in the midst and asked Jesus, saying, "Do You answer nothing? What *is it* these men testify against You?" 61 But He kept silent and answered nothing.

LUKE 22: 66 As soon as it was day, the elders of the people, both chief priests and scribes, came together and led Him into their council, saying, 67 "If You are the Christ, tell us."

But He said to them, "If I tell you, you will by no means believe. 68 And if I also ask *you,* you will by no means answer Me or let *Me* go. 69 Hereafter the Son of Man will sit on the right hand of the power of God."

70 Then they all said, "Are You then the Son of God?"

So He said to them, "You *rightly* say that I am."

71 And they said, "What further testimony do we need? For we have heard it ourselves from His own mouth." MARK 14:64 You have heard the blasphemy! What do you think?"

And they all condemned Him to be deserving of death.

65 Then some began to spit on Him, and to blindfold Him, and to beat Him, and to say to Him, "Prophesy!" And the officers struck Him with the palms of their hands.

66 Now as Peter was below in the courtyard, one of the servant girls of the high priest came. 67 And when she saw Peter warming himself, she looked at him and said, "You also were with Jesus of Nazareth."

68 But he denied it, saying, "I neither know nor understand what you are saying." And he went out on the porch, and a rooster crowed.

69 And the servant girl saw him again, and began to say to those who stood by, "This is one of them." 70 But he denied it again.

And a little later those who stood by said to Peter again, "Surely you are *one* of them; for you are a Galilean, and your speech shows *it.*"

⁷¹ Then he began to curse and swear, "I do not know this Man of whom you speak!"

⁷² A second time *the* rooster crowed. Then Peter called to mind the word that Jesus had said to him, "Before the rooster crows twice, you will deny Me three times." And when he thought about it, he wept.

13/ Judas' Despair

MATTHEW 27:3 Then Judas, His betrayer, seeing that He had been condemned, was remorseful and brought back the thirty pieces of silver to the chief priests and elders, ⁴ saying, "I have sinned by betraying innocent blood."

And they said, "What *is that* to us? You see *to it!*"

⁵ Then he threw down the pieces of silver in the temple and departed, and went and hanged himself.

⁶ But the chief priests took the silver pieces and said, "It is not lawful to put them into the treasury, because they are the price of blood." ⁷ And they consulted together and bought with them the potter's field, to bury strangers in. ⁸ Therefore that field has been called the Field of Blood to this day.

⁹ Then was fulfilled what was spoken by Jeremiah the prophet, saying, *"And they took the thirty pieces of silver, the value of Him who was priced,* whom they of the children of Israel priced, ¹⁰ *and* gave them for the potter's field, as the LORD directed me."

14/ Jesus First Appearance Before Pilate

Jerusalem, Praetorium (Roman Headquarters, Northwest corner of the Temple Mount)

JOHN 18:28 Then they led Jesus from Caiaphas to the Praetorium, and it was early morning. But they themselves did not go into the Praetorium, lest they should be defiled, but that they might eat the Passover. ²⁹ Pilate then went out to them and said, "What accusation do you bring against this Man?"

³⁰ They answered and said to him, "If He were not an evildoer, we would not have delivered Him up to you."

³¹ Then Pilate said to them, "You take Him and judge Him according to your law."

Therefore the Jews said to him, "It is not lawful for us to put anyone to death," ³² that the saying of Jesus might be fulfilled which He spoke, signifying by what death He would die.

LUKE 23:2 And they began to accuse Him, saying, "We found this *fellow* perverting the nation, and forbidding to pay taxes to Caesar, saying that He Himself is Christ, a King."

JOHN 18:33 Then Pilate entered the Praetorium again, called Jesus, and said to Him, "Are You the King of the Jews?"

³⁴ Jesus answered him, "Are you speaking for yourself about this, or did others tell you this concerning Me?"

³⁵ Pilate answered, "Am I a Jew? Your own nation and the chief priests have delivered You to me. What have You done?"

³⁶ Jesus answered, "My kingdom is not of this world. If My kingdom were of this world, My servants would fight, so that I should not be delivered to the Jews; but now My kingdom is not from here."

³⁷ Pilate therefore said to Him, "Are You a king then?"

Jesus answered, "You say *rightly* that I am a king. For this cause I was born, and for this cause I have come into the world, that I should bear witness to the truth. Everyone who is of the truth hears My voice." MATTHEW 27:11B "*It is as* you say." ¹² And while He was being accused by the chief priests and elders, He answered nothing.

¹³ Then Pilate said to Him, "Do You not hear how many things they testify against You?" ¹⁴ But He answered him not one word, so that the governor marveled greatly.

LUKE 23:4 So Pilate said to the chief priests and the crowd, "I find no fault in this Man."

⁵ But they were the more fierce, saying, "He stirs up the people, teaching throughout all Judea, beginning from Galilee to this place."

15/ Pilate Sends Jesus to Herod
Jerusalem, Herod's Palace

LUKE 23:6 When Pilate heard of Galilee, he asked if the Man were a Galilean. ⁷ And as soon as he knew that He belonged to Herod's jurisdiction, he sent Him to Herod, who was also in Jerusalem at that time.

⁸ Now when Herod saw Jesus, he was exceedingly glad; for he had desired for a long *time* to see Him, because he had heard many things about Him, and he hoped to see some miracle done by Him. ⁹ Then he questioned Him with many words, but He answered him nothing. ¹⁰ And the chief priests and scribes stood and vehemently accused Him. ¹¹ Then Herod, with his men of war, treated Him with contempt and mocked *Him,* arrayed Him in a gorgeous robe, and sent Him back to Pilate. ¹² That very day Pilate and Herod became friends with each other, for previously they had been at enmity with each other.

16/ Jesus' Second Appearance before Pilate
Jerusalem, Praetorium

LUKE 23:13 Then Pilate, when he had called together the chief priests, the rulers, and the people, ¹⁴ said to them, "You have brought this Man to me, as one who misleads the people. And indeed, having examined *Him* in your presence, I have found no fault in this Man concerning those things of which you accuse Him; ¹⁵ no, neither did Herod, for I sent you back to him; and indeed nothing deserving of death has been done by Him. ¹⁶ I will therefore chastise Him and release *Him*"

MATTHEW 27:15 Now at the feast the governor was accustomed to releasing to the multitude one prisoner whom they wished. ¹⁶ And at that time they had a notorious prisoner called Barabbas. ¹⁷ Therefore, when they had gathered together, Pilate said to them, "Whom do you want me to release to you? Barabbas, or Jesus who is called Christ?" ¹⁸ For he knew that they had handed Him over because of envy.

¹⁹ While he was sitting on the judgment seat, his wife sent to him, saying, "Have nothing to do with that just Man, for I have suffered many things today in a dream because of Him."

²⁰ But the chief priests and elders persuaded the multitudes that they should ask for Barabbas and destroy Jesus. ²¹ The governor answered and said to them, "Which of the two do you want me to release to you?"

LUKE 23:18 And they all cried out at once, saying, "Away with this *Man*, and release to us Barabbas"—¹⁹ who had been thrown into prison for a certain rebellion made in the city, and for murder.

²⁰ Pilate, therefore, wishing to release Jesus, again called out to them. ²¹ But they shouted, saying, "Crucify *Him*, crucify Him!"

²² Then he said to them the third time, "Why, what evil has He done? I have found no reason for death in Him. I will therefore chastise Him and let *Him* go."

²³ But they were insistent, demanding with loud voices that He be crucified. And the voices of these men and of the chief priests prevailed.

17/ "Behold the Man!"

JOHN 19:1 So then Pilate took Jesus and scourged *Him*. MATTHEW 27:27 Then the soldiers of the governor took Jesus into the Praetorium and gathered the whole garrison around Him. ²⁸ And they stripped Him and put a scarlet robe on Him. ²⁹ When they had twisted a crown of thorns, they put *it* on His head, and a reed in His right hand. And they bowed the knee before Him and mocked Him, saying, "Hail, King of the Jews!" ³⁰ Then they spat on Him, and took the reed and struck Him on the head. ᴶᴼᴴᴺ ¹⁹:³ᴮ And they struck Him with their hands. ᴹᴬᵀᵀᴴᴱᵂ ²⁷:³¹ And when they had mocked Him, ᴶᴼᴴᴺ ¹⁹:⁴ Pilate then went out again, and said to them, "Behold, I am bringing Him out to you, that you may know that I find no fault in Him."

⁵ Then Jesus came out, wearing the crown of thorns and the purple robe. And *Pilate* said to them, "Behold the Man!"

⁶ Therefore, when the chief priests and officers saw Him, they cried out, saying, "Crucify *Him,* crucify *Him!*"

Pilate said to them, "You take Him and crucify *Him,* for I find no fault in Him."

⁷ The Jews answered him, "We have a law, and according to our law He ought to die, because He made Himself the Son of God."

⁸ Therefore, when Pilate heard that saying, he was the more afraid, ⁹ and went again into the Praetorium, and said to Jesus, "Where are You from?" But Jesus gave him no answer.

¹⁰ Then Pilate said to Him, "Are You not speaking to me? Do You not know that I have power to crucify You, and power to release You?"

¹¹ Jesus answered, "You could have no power at all against Me unless it had been given you from above. Therefore the one who delivered Me to you has the greater sin."

¹² From then on Pilate sought to release Him, but the Jews cried out, saying, "If you let this Man go, you are not Caesar's friend. Whoever makes himself a king speaks against Caesar."

¹³ When Pilate therefore heard that saying, he brought Jesus out and sat down in the judgment seat in a place that is called *The* Pavement, but in Hebrew, Gabbatha. ¹⁴ Now it was the Preparation Day of the Passover, and about the sixth hour. And he said to the Jews, "Behold your King!"

¹⁵ But they cried out, "Away with *Him,* away with *Him!* Crucify Him!"

Pilate said to them, "Shall I crucify your King?"

The chief priests answered, "We have no king but Caesar!"

18/ Pilate Delivers Jesus to Be Crucified

ᴹᴬᵀᵀᴴᴱᵂ ²⁷:²⁴ When Pilate saw that he could not prevail at all, but rather *that* a tumult was rising, he took water and washed *his* hands before the multitude, saying, "I am innocent of the blood of this just Person. You see *to it.*"

²⁵ And all the people answered and said, "His blood *be* on us and on our children."

19/The Way to Golgotha
From the Governor's Palace, through the city, outside the gate of Jerusalem, Golgotha

MARK 15:20 And when they had mocked Him, they took the purple off Him, put His own clothes on Him, and led Him out to crucify Him.

[21] Then they compelled a certain man, Simon a Cyrenian, the father of Alexander and Rufus, as he was coming out of the country and passing by, to bear His cross.

LUKE 23:27 And a great multitude of the people followed Him, and women who also mourned and lamented Him. [28] But Jesus, turning to them, said, "Daughters of Jerusalem, do not weep for Me, but weep for yourselves and for your children. [29] For indeed the days are coming in which they will say, 'Blessed *are* the barren, wombs that never bore, and breasts which never nursed!' [30] Then they will begin '*to say to the mountains, "Fall on us!" and to the hills, "Cover us!"*' [31] For if they do these things in the green wood, what will be done in the dry?"

[32] There were also two others, criminals, led with Him to be put to death.

20/ The Crucifixion
Golgotha

MARK 15:22 And they brought Him to the place Golgotha, which is translated, Place of a Skull. [23] Then they gave Him wine mingled with myrrh to drink, but He did not take *it.*

LUKE 23: 32 There were also two others, criminals, led with Him to be put to death. [33] And when they had come to the place called Calvary, there they crucified Him, and the criminals, one on the right hand and the other on the left. [34] Then Jesus said, "Father, forgive them, for they do not know what they do."

JOHN 19:17 And He, bearing His cross, went out to a place called *the Place* of a Skull, which is called in Hebrew, Golgotha, [18] where they crucified Him, and two others with Him, one on either side, and Jesus in the center. [19] Now Pilate wrote a title and put *it* on the cross. And the writing was:

JESUS OF NAZARETH, THE KING OF THE JEWS

[20] Then many of the Jews read this title, for the place where Jesus was crucified was near the city; and it was written in Hebrew, Greek, *and* Latin.

[21] Therefore the chief priests of the Jews said to Pilate, "Do not write, 'The King of the Jews,' but, 'He said, "I am the King of the Jews."'"

[22] Pilate answered, "What I have written, I have written."

[23] Then the soldiers, when they had crucified Jesus, took His garments and made four parts, to each soldier a part, and also the tunic. Now the tunic was

without seam, woven from the top in one piece. ²⁴ They said therefore among themselves, "Let us not tear it, but cast lots for it, whose it shall be," that the Scripture might be fulfilled which says:

"They divided My garments among them,
And for My clothing they cast lots."

Therefore the soldiers did these things.

²⁵ Now there stood by the cross of Jesus His mother, and His mother's sister, Mary the *wife* of Clopas, and Mary Magdalene. ²⁶ When Jesus therefore saw His mother, and the disciple whom He loved standing by, He said to His mother, "Woman, behold your son!" ²⁷ Then He said to the disciple, "Behold your mother!" And from that hour that disciple took her to his own *home*.

MATTHEW 27:38 Then two robbers were crucified with Him, one on the right and another on the left.

³⁹ And those who passed by blasphemed Him, wagging their heads ⁴⁰ and saying, "You who destroy the temple and build *it* in three days, save Yourself! If You are the Son of God, come down from the cross."

⁴¹ Likewise the chief priests also, mocking with the scribes and elders, said, ⁴² "He saved others; Himself He cannot save. If He is the King of Israel, let Him now come down from the cross, and we will believe Him. ⁴³ He trusted in God; let Him deliver Him now if He will have Him; for He said, 'I am the Son of God.'"

LUKE 23:39 Then one of the criminals who were hanged blasphemed Him, saying, "If You are the Christ, save Yourself and us."

⁴⁰ But the other, answering, rebuked him, saying, "Do you not even fear God, seeing you are under the same condemnation? ⁴¹ And we indeed justly, for we receive the due reward of our deeds; but this Man has done nothing wrong." ⁴² Then he said to Jesus, "Lord, remember me when You come into Your kingdom."

⁴³ And Jesus said to him, "Assuredly, I say to you, today you will be with Me in Paradise."

MATTHEW 27:45 Now from the sixth hour until the ninth hour there was darkness over all the land. ⁴⁶ And about the ninth hour Jesus cried out with a loud voice, saying, "Eli, Eli, lama sabachthani?" that is, *"My God, My God, why have You forsaken Me?"*

⁴⁷ Some of those who stood there, when they heard *that,* said, "This Man is calling for Elijah!"

JOHN 19:28 After this, Jesus, knowing that all things were now accomplished, that the Scripture might be fulfilled, said, "I thirst!" ²⁹ Now a vessel full of sour wine was sitting there; and they filled a sponge with sour wine, put *it* on hyssop, and put *it* to His mouth. MATTHEW 27:49 The rest said, "Let Him alone; let us see if Elijah will come to save Him."

JOHN 19:30 So when Jesus had received the sour wine, He said, "It is finished!"

LUKE 23:46 And when Jesus had cried out with a loud voice, He said, "Father, *'into Your hands I commit My spirit.'*" Having said this, He breathed His last.

JOHN 19:30B And bowing His head, He gave up His spirit.

MATTHEW 27:51 Then, behold, the veil of the temple was torn in two from top to bottom; and the earth quaked, and the rocks were split, 52 and the graves were opened; and many bodies of the saints who had fallen asleep were raised; 53 and coming out of the graves after His resurrection, they went into the holy city and appeared to many.

54 So when the centurion and those with him, who were guarding Jesus, saw the earthquake and the things that had happened, they feared greatly, saying, "Truly this was the Son of God!" LUKE 23:47B "Certainly this was a righteous Man!"

48 And the whole crowd who came together to that sight, seeing what had been done, beat their breasts and returned. 49 But all His acquaintances, and the women who followed Him from Galilee, stood at a distance, watching these things. MARK 15:40 There were also women looking on from afar, among whom were Mary Magdalene, Mary the mother of James the Less and of Joses, and Salome, 41 who also followed Him and ministered to Him when He was in Galilee, and many other women who came up with Him to Jerusalem.

21/ Jesus' Side Pierced

JOHN 19:31 Therefore, because it was the Preparation *Day,* that the bodies should not remain on the cross on the Sabbath (for that Sabbath was a high day), the Jews asked Pilate that their legs might be broken, and *that* they might be taken away. 32 Then the soldiers came and broke the legs of the first and of the other who was crucified with Him. 33 But when they came to Jesus and saw that He was already dead, they did not break His legs. 34 But one of the soldiers pierced His side with a spear, and immediately blood and water came out. 35 And he who has seen has testified, and his testimony is true; and he knows that he is telling the truth, so that you may believe. 36 For these things were done that the Scripture should be fulfilled, *"Not one of His bones shall be broken."* 37 And again another Scripture says, *"They shall look on Him whom they pierced."*

22/Burial of Jesus
The Tomb in the Garden, close to Golgotha

MARK 15:42 Now when evening had come, because it was the Preparation Day, that is, the day before the Sabbath, ⁴³ Joseph of Arimathea, a prominent council member, who was himself waiting for the kingdom of God, coming and taking courage, went in to Pilate and asked for the body of Jesus. ⁴⁴ Pilate marveled that He was already dead; and summoning the centurion, he asked him if He had been dead for some time. ⁴⁵ So when he found out from the centurion, he granted the body to Joseph. ⁴⁶ Then he bought fine linen, took Him down, and wrapped Him in the linen. JOHN 19:39 And Nicodemus, who at first came to Jesus by night, also came, bringing a mixture of myrrh and aloes, about a hundred pounds. ⁴⁰ Then they took the body of Jesus, and bound it in strips of linen with the spices, as the custom of the Jews is to bury. ⁴¹ Now in the place where He was crucified there was a garden, and in the garden a new tomb in which no one had yet been laid. ⁴² So there they laid Jesus, because of the Jews' Preparation *Day,* for the tomb was nearby. MARK 15:46B And he laid Him in a tomb which had been hewn out of the rock, and rolled a stone against the door of the tomb. ⁴⁷ And Mary Magdalene and Mary *the mother* of Joses observed where He was laid.

LUKE 23: 55 And the women who had come with Him from Galilee followed after, and they observed the tomb and how His body was laid.⁵⁶ Then they returned and prepared spices and fragrant oils. And they rested on the Sabbath according to the commandment.

MATTHEW 27:62 On the next day, which followed the Day of Preparation, the chief priests and Pharisees gathered together to Pilate, ⁶³ saying, "Sir, we remember, while He was still alive, how that deceiver said, 'After three days I will rise.' ⁶⁴ Therefore command that the tomb be made secure until the third day, lest His disciples come by night and steal Him *away,* and say to the people, 'He has risen from the dead.' So the last deception will be worse than the first."

⁶⁵ Pilate said to them, "You have a guard; go your way, make *it* as secure as you know how." ⁶⁶ So they went and made the tomb secure, sealing the stone and setting the guard.

Made in the USA
Middletown, DE
31 January 2024

48426756R00052